P R

AMERICA
FOR THE
WRATH
OF
GOD

PREPARING
AMERICA
FOR THE
WRATH
OF
GOD

WOODROW L. POLSTON

CREATION
HOUSE

PREPARING AMERICA FOR THE WRATH OF GOD
by Woodrow Polston
Published by Creation House
A Charisma Media Company
600 Rinehart Road
Lake Mary, Florida 32746
www.charismamedia.com

Unless otherwise noted, all Scripture quotations are from the King James Version of the Bible.

Scripture quotations marked NKJV are from the New King James Version of the Bible. Copyright © 1979, 1980, 1982 by Thomas Nelson, Inc., publishers. Used by permission.

Scripture quotations marked NAS are from the New American Standard Bible. Copyright © 1960, 1962, 1963, 1968, 1971, 1972, 1973, 1975, 1977, 1995 by the Lockman Foundation. Used by permission. (www.Lockman.org)

All quotations from the Apocrypha are from the Revised Standard Version of the Bible. Copyright © 1946, 1952, 1971 by the Division of Christian Education of the National Council of the Churches of Christ in the USA. Used by permission.

All quotations from the Quran are from the Authorized English Version, Copyright © 2007 Book of Signs Foundation.

Author photo courtesy of Edwin Rader.

Design Director: Bill Johnson
Cover design by Lisa Cox

Visit the author's website: http://gearsofprophecy.com

Library of Congress Cataloging-in-Publication Data:
2013937680
International Standard Book Number: 978-1-62136-371-2
E-book International Standard Book Number:
978-1-62136-372-9

While the author has made every effort to provide accurate
telephone numbers and Internet addresses at the time of
publication, neither the publisher nor the author assumes
any responsibility for errors or for changes that occur after
publication.

13 14 15 16 17 — 9 8 7 6 5 4 3 2
Printed in the United States of America

DEDICATION

I dedicate this book to all the loving and supporting members of my family. And most especially to Jim Talley.

TABLE OF CONTENTS

PREFACE

FROM THE VERY birth of our nation, formed by Christian men, God has used America to fulfill prophecy. A few worthy quotes from these men are as follows:

> To the distinguished character of Patriot, it should be our highest glory to add the more distinguished character of Christian.
>
> —GEORGE WASHINGTON
> FIRST PRESIDENT OF THE UNITED STATES

> God who gave us life gave us liberty. And can the liberties of a nation be thought secure when we have removed their only firm basis?
>
> —THOMAS JEFFERSON
> THIRD PRESIDENT OF THE UNITED STATES

> Resistance to tyranny becomes the Christian and social duty of each individual. Continue steadfast and with a proper sense of your dependence on God, nobly defend those rights which heaven gave, and no man ought to take from us.
>
> —JOHN HANCOCK, FIRST SIGNER OF THE
> DECLARATION OF INDEPENDENCE

It wasn't long before missions work started in America to spread the Word of God across the entire world. On February 19, 1812, Adoniram Judson left for India as the first American missionary. One year later, he found himself in Burma and devoted his life to bringing the gospel to the Burmese people. It took him six years to see his first convert, and he buried three wives on the mission field, all to plant seeds for a great harvest in Burma. Since that very first mission from the nation of America, countless people around the world have not only received the Word of God, but have also been fed, clothed, cared for, and treated with medicines.

As a young nation and ultimately a new world, America helped foreign countries come to God through its missions work, and immigrants from many countries became Christians through its way of life. God was everywhere—in churches, in schools, in the workplace.

Sadly, today you won't find Him in schools, the workplace, and in some cases not even in church! The early American Christian family was devoted to God and had a very high moral standard and honest way of life. Business was not conducted on Sundays, nor was labor performed, in order to keep the Sabbath holy. A neighbor was there for you if you needed help, food, or any kind of support. Today, a good neighbor is hard to find, and a neighbor is often someone with whom you get caught up in lawsuits and domestic disputes.

I recall seeing a large Bible from the 1880s that had a "pledge page" in it for all family members to sign. It was meant for pledging to not partake in the consumption of alcohol, and it stated there were an estimated 300,000 alcoholics in England at that time. Look at us today! And if only alcohol was our biggest problem! Fast forward a little over a century later, and we have a never-ending list of drugs, narcotics both illegal and legitimate, that are highly addictive. These drugs have come into schools and suburban areas, whereas before they were only obtainable in the inner cities. They are not only pushed by thug drug dealers but also by doctors, and all sources of media.

Looking back on the course of American history, one might say all was fine and then someone let the devil in. Basically, that is what happened, and a close, detailed look will reveal the stepping stones throughout our history that brought us to become what a prophet from the days of the Bible would call a "Sodom and Gomorrah" nation.

Chapter 1

1948

I T IS MY opinion and the opinion of many scholars that the most important prophecy to be fulfilled in our life-time—and possibly since the life, crucifixion, and res-urrection of Jesus Christ—was the rebirth of the nation of Israel. It recalls the prophecy from Ezekiel 37:

> Then He said to me, "Son of man, these bones are the whole house of Israel. They indeed say, 'Our bones are dry, our hope is lost, and we ourselves are cut off!' Therefore prophesy and say to them, 'Thus says the Lord God: "Behold, O My people, I will open your graves and cause you to come up from your graves, and bring you into the land of Israel. Then you shall know that I am the Lord, when I have opened your graves, O My people, and brought you up from your graves. I will put My Spirit in you, and you shall live, and I will place you in your own land. Then you shall know

that I, the LORD, have spoken it and performed it,"
says the LORD.'"

—vv. 11–14, NKJV

On May 14, 1948, the state of Israel was declared a
nation. America had a large hand in helping this come
to pass. Many believe that this event triggered the fast-
paced ticking of the prophetic time clock quoted by Jesus:
"Now learn a parable of the fig tree; When his branch is
yet tender, and putteth forth leaves, ye know that summer
is nigh: So likewise ye, when ye shall see all these things,
know that it is near, even at the doors. Verily I say unto
you, This generation shall not pass, till all these things be
fulfilled" (Matt. 24:32–34).

Is it safe to say that our day-to-day life has been spin-
ning out of control since this prophecy came to pass? The
answer is without any doubt, yes!

Let's take a look at the birth of a music genre that promoted rebellion nationwide and made idols of many: rock
'n' roll. It is debated among many the exact year that the
sensation was born. Some say it was 1935, when Elvis
Presley was born, but others say it was the early 1950s.

What is the main instrument that has always been the
key ingredient to rock 'n' roll music? The answer is the
electric guitar. The most important product for rock 'n'
roll music was first invented by California instrument
maker Leo Fender in 1948. Therefore, many believe the
birth of rock 'n' roll was, in fact, 1948.

The beginning of rock 'n' roll was subtle in its rebellion.
It quickly became the preferred music of the youth of the
nation. We can cover many topics that link moral decline
to rock 'n' roll music—such as its progressive trend toward
Satanism, substance abuse, and suicide—and we will. But

let's first look at some other signs of the times as they relate to this prophetic year.

THE AMERICAN GAY RIGHTS MOVEMENT

In 1948, a man named Alfred Kinsey published a book titled *Sexual Behavior in the Human Male*. In this book, Kinsey revealed to the public that homosexuality is far more widespread and common than believed. His studies on sexual behavior are considered to be, by some, the start of the sexual revolution. He later went on to publish *Sexual Behavior in the Human Female*.

Only three years later, in 1951, the first national gay rights organization was formed. Its founder, Harry Hay, is considered the founder of the gay rights movement. In 1955, the first lesbian rights organization was formed in San Francisco. Illinois became the first state in the US to decriminalize homosexual acts in 1962.

As we Christians know, homosexuality is an abomination, and it should be shunned as well as preached against. Far too often, a Christian is considered a hateful person for speaking out against homosexuality. While there *are* people out there who hate gays, true Christians do not hate the people who are gay but rather the act and lifestyle of a gay person. This lifestyle is hated by Christians because it is clearly a forbidden sin.

I am always surprised to meet people who support gay rights but aren't gay themselves. Christians are seen as "oppressive people" for our views, but we are the ones who will needlessly suffer the wrath of God, along with every gay person and gay rights supporter, in the event of a destructive judgment on our nation! Does this not make clear sense to you: *If you support gay rights and gay marriage, you will be judged for encouraging sin.* Are supporters really willing to suffer judgment for something they didn't personally partake in? If you support smoking cigarettes, are you willing to share the cancer of the smoker? If someone tells you they are going to rob a bank and you say, "Go for it," would you be willing to share their prison sentence? I think not.

Let's take a look at the Scriptures concerning these things. Some relevant passages include:

> Thou shalt not lie with mankind, as with woman-kind: it is abomination.
>
> —LEVITICUS 18:22

> And likewise also the men, leaving the natural use of the woman, burned in their lust one toward another, men with men working that which is unseemly, and receiving in themselves that rec-ompence of their error which was met.
>
> —ROMANS 1:27

And let us not forget Sodom and Gomorrah, which was destroyed for homosexuality and fornication. Most everyone is aware that there is a disease—or a plague, if you will—that is contracted through sexual intercourse called the AIDS virus. If you ask most people when it first appeared, they will tell you it was in the early '80s. In fact, the disease was first discovered in 1959, when a man died from it in the Congo.

What is most unfortunate for people who support gay rights is the "bisexual factor." Many people in American society have labeled themselves with this term. They participate in sexual acts with both sexes, and it goes without saying that they are active with many different partners.

So let's imagine you are a young woman who supports gay rights but aren't yourself gay, and your new boyfriend is bisexual. It is very likely he may have had relations with a gay man who had AIDS. This disease can be contracted and go undetected for years. Are you really willing to risk your life for the sake of another person's sin? The fact of the matter is that when a sin is repeated over and over and becomes a way of life, it is iniquity, and God remembers iniquity and casts a destructive judgment because of it.

God created man and woman; there is a covenant between them. To God, a covenant is a contract not to be broken. Yet all across America, the contract has been disregarded. Imagine for a moment if every homeowner in the country decided to no longer recognize their mortgage contract. What do you think would happen? They would lose their homes and have no one to blame but themselves. And who could blame the mortgage company?

SATANISM AND THE OCCULT

Our Lady of Endor Coven, also known as *Ophite Cultus Satanas*, was the first recognized satanic cult in America, founded in 1948 by Herbert Arthur Sloane in Toledo, Ohio. This group worshipped Satan, whom they recognized as the serpent in the Garden of Eden.

While many cults have come and gone in America, the atmosphere opened up over our nation to welcome in demonic forces. In 1966, the Church of Satan was established in San Francisco by Anton LaVey, who was also the high priest of the church. He died in 1997, and those appointed to take over moved the church headquarters to New York City. Throughout the years, the church has worked to promote itself through film, music, and other means of self-promotion. As of 2012, the church is still very much alive but will not disclose how many members it contains.

You may be shocked to learn that Satanists don't actually worship Satan—or even believe in his existence, for that matter! They do not believe in God, the devil, or any spiritual being whatsoever. According to their beliefs, Satanism is just a way of life, a mode of behavior. There are nine satanic sins, the first of which is *stupidity*. I have to stop there—I won't waste our time! We have to consider such people as extremely confused, to say the least! Would you call yourself a Christian if you didn't believe Christ ever existed?

Obviously it would take strong delusions of the mind for someone to think Satan is on their side or that he has their best interest in mind. Satan failed to worship God in heaven, which was his job as "the anointed cherub." He waged a war in heaven and failed. In doing so, one-third of the angels were cast out of heaven with him.

When God created man, Satan became furious. Man was created in God's image, so if Satan hates God, consider for a moment how he feels about mankind, which is the reflection of God. Satan will most certainly drag down as many people with him as he can.

Many Americans today turn to horoscopes, psychics, and other various types of readings for answers—and they pay good money for them, when they could speak to God, who created all things, for free. Mediums who are open to spirits welcome demons through channeling and other rituals. And they can, in fact, give answers to those who ask questions, but at what price? Now you have a demon that knows things about you and, more than likely, is going to hang around and haunt your steps.

It is my belief that ghosts and hauntings are actually demons and evil spirits: "For the living know that they shall die: but the dead know not any thing, neither have they any more a reward; for the memory of them is forgotten" (Eccles. 9:5). I may be wrong on this theory, but if ghosts are, in fact, demons playing games with us, we should certainly look at the subject in a different light. We may be entertaining demons in our quest to catch a ghost. In either case, we are occupying ourselves with something otherworldly, and it is certainly a distraction from our purpose in life and what God wants us to be doing with our precious time on earth.

UFOs and Secret Technology

On July 8, 1947, the Roswell Army Air Field public information officer, Walter Haut, in Roswell, New Mexico, issued a press release stating that personnel from the field's 509th bomb unit had recovered a crashed flying disc from a ranch near Roswell, sparking intense media interest. Later that day, the commanding general said it was a radar-tracking balloon.

This event gave birth to a never-ending list of government conspiracies, including the cover-up of alien spacecraft, alien bodies, alien technology, and more. As the years have gone by, we have only seen the phenomenon increase. With cameras and video recorders now everywhere and in the hands of potential eyewitnesses, we have seen many pieces of evidence that certainly appear to be otherworldly. And while many put their absolute faith in the existence of alien beings, who are visiting Earth from other planets out of their concern for our well-being, there is a growing theory that these are actually demons who drop in on us under the deception of being from another planet.

Could such beings be comparable to the sons of God, or the nephilim, who are briefly described in the Book of Genesis? Could the technology we have today be credited to a higher intelligence, such as fallen angels? It is certainly interesting that we witnessed such a sudden increase in knowledge and technology around this time period. Many now believe that the strange crafts seen in the sky is secret technology developed and operated by the government. Conspiracy theorists in the Christian community believe the government will use an alien-abduction scenario to ease the public in an event such as the Rapture.

THE BIRTH OF A NEW GOD: TELEVISION

In 1947, there were an estimated 40 million radios in homes across America and only about 44,000 television sets. Of those 44,000, it is estimated that 30,000 were in New York alone. By 1948, CBS and ABC had been established, and by 1949, the networks stretched from New York to the Mississippi River, then all the way to the West Coast by 1951.[1] It wasn't long before American families found themselves coming together like a congregation to sit in silence, as though hypnotized, in front of the "picture box."

With its more than seventy years of existence in our homes, the television has been a very useful tool in keeping us up to date. We follow world events as well as local news. We can get an accurate forecast for weather conditions and so much more. We certainly cannot deny that many people have come to God through televised evangelism and Christian programs that teach the Bible.

But throughout the years, television sitcoms have

numbed the minds of Americans and have progressively become immoral. Today it is common to view a sitcom that promotes sexual promiscuity, homosexuality, self-glorification, and just about any other sin you can imagine. With television came many new opportunities to turn our attention from God. In 1972, the first video-game console that connected to the TV was the Odyssey, released by Magnavox. Today, we have a large variety of game systems and an endless list of games to choose from.

A recent survey found that in 67 percent of homes, the TV is on during meals; in 49 percent of homes, the TV is on most of the time, even when no one is watching it.[2] When children go to their rooms, media still surrounds them, with the survey finding that almost 80 percent of household youths have a TV in their room,[3] and 50 percent of children aged 0–8 years and 83 percent of children aged 8–18 years have a gaming console attached to their TV.[4] Another survey found that among teens and young adults, nearly eight hours of each day is dedicated to media,[5] with some being so devoted to their games that they wear an adult diaper so as not to interrupt their session.[6]

Then came the video industry, which is certainly worse than the game system. On November 11, 1951, the electronics division of Bing Crosby Enterprises gave the world's first demonstration of a videotape recording in Los Angeles. But it wasn't until 1975 that the videocassette recorder was mass-produced. Since videocassettes, we have advanced to digital versatile discs, or DVDs.

With pornography being debated in courtrooms in the early 1970s, it was born and has since become a multi-billion-dollar industry in America today. With stores popping up everywhere to sell adult films and other novelties, men and women alike have been drawn into its soulless entertainment. It has caused many divorces, the separation of families, the spreading of disease, and ultimately the corruption of the masses. Many Americans today label themselves "porn addicts," some of whom have to go through rehab programs to cleanse their thoughts of the images etched in their minds.

Without any doubt, we can see that a lot of interesting things started happening in history around the year 1948 that would change our everyday lives. It is also notable that the world's twelfth deadliest earthquake occurred in 1948, on October 6, in Ashgabat, a region of Iran, killing more than 110,000 people.[7]

Chapter 2

THE LONG ROAD TO
THE WRATH OF GOD

THANKFULLY FOR OUR sake, and the sake of all flesh, God is slow to anger. But when He has had enough, the results are always of biblical proportions. As the Book of Numbers teaches, "The LORD is longsuffering, and of great mercy, forgiving iniquity and transgression, and by no means clearing the guilty, visiting the iniquity of the fathers upon the children unto the third and fourth generation" (Num. 14:18).

We have been a blessed nation, far better off than many others. We have been spoiled with many freedoms that we often take for granted. For example, in many Arab countries, you can be executed for your religious beliefs. Thieves can expect to have a hand chopped off, and an adulteress can be stoned to death.

Personally, I thank God every day for His blessings, as I'm sure many of you do. But when the majority in our country has stopped doing so, we as a nation become like ungrateful children, in pursuit of our own desires, waking up each day to do what pleases ourselves rather than the will of God.

A common argument from agnostic people is that God of the Bible is just too harsh in His judgment, but a good point can be made from this statement. If you consider for a moment our laws and judgments in America, when a person is identified as having committed a crime, they are immediately arrested, prosecuted, and judged. There is no judge in America who will hear a criminal ask forgiveness and then set him free.

We must keep in mind that our sins have been continual as a nation for many years now, and we have yet to see a fitting judgment.

> In the measure that she glorified herself and lived luxuriously, in the same measure give her torment and sorrow; for she says in her heart, "I sit as queen, and am no widow, and will not see sorrow."
> —REVELATION 18:7, NKJV

If we are to be judged in the same measure of our blessings and sins, we are in big trouble. Let's break down this verse from Revelation and see how it can be directly applied to our nation, more so than any other.

"She glorified herself and lived luxuriously." The most factual piece of evidence for this statement is revealed through our film and music industry. If you look up the word *glorified* in the dictionary, you will find its definition is "to cause to be, or treat as being more splendid, excellent, etc., than would normally be considered." Our films have a worldwide audience, and so many of them paint a deceptive picture of American life. Action films always have a

soldier or a secret agent that is utterly indestructible, while Russian President Dmitry Medvedev said in a recent interview that he wished we wouldn't so often portray Russians as "bad guys."[1] So commonly, you see average American families in films living in gigantic homes, driving $60,000 cars, and having every possible piece of technology at their disposal. This is why it is shocking to learn that one in every six Americans live in poverty.[2]

In music videos, we see rap artists wearing $20,000 necklaces and $10,000 watches as they lay poolside and brag about having every luxury available to them. They often claim they've stayed true to their humble beginnings, coming from project areas and bad city streets, but the only evidence of this is that they continue to promote crime and drug use, rather than speaking out against them, or using their fortunes to fund programs to improve the bad environments from which they came.

We must also consider the world of cosmetic surgery. With millions of makeup and hair products on the market, many go far beyond their use. Undergoing knife and laser for the sake of glorifying one's self, Americans spend more than $10 billion a year on procedures such as face lifts and breast implants, despite the country being in a recession.[3]

"I sit as queen, and am no widow, and will not see sorrow." On July 4, 1776, the thirteen American colonies declared their independence from Great Britain and King George III. Therefore, we sit as a queen and, never having had a king, we are no widow. But are we of the opinion that we will see no sorrow? If ever there was a country to feel safe and secure, it was certainly America—that is, until the events of a terrorist attack played out on September 11, 2001. In this event, we witnessed the destruction of the World Trade Center in New York City, as well as damage

to the Pentagon in Washington, DC, and the casualty of more than 3,000 American lives.

On September 20, 2001, President George W. Bush declared the war on terror. On October 7, 2001, US and British forces invaded Afghanistan and began the hunt for Osama bin Laden, the mastermind behind the attacks. Then on March 20, 2003, the United States invaded the country of Iraq. Having intelligence information that Saddam Hussein was in possession of weapons of mass destruction, we further assured ourselves that we would see no sorrow brought upon us by the hands of a madman.

Since the war on terror was declared, we have been subjected to many new laws and losses of liberty, all in the name of security. With many American citizens willing to give up rights, be patted down and inspected at airports, and be considered "suspect" when snapping photos or filming national monuments, we can at least sleep at night, knowing that all steps are being taken to assure no sorrow will befall us. But as the Bible indicates, we will certainly suffer many sorrows. And the possibilities are building up like dark, ominous clouds.

As the country's sinful way of life has continued through the generations, we have continued our travel down the road to hell and to the wrath of God. And sadly, there are multitudes of people, gridlocked in a huge traffic jam as far as the eye can see, anxious to get there. A very sobering Bible verse that should shake anyone comes to mind: "Hell from beneath is excited about you, to meet you at your coming" (Isa. 14:9, NKJV).

POWERS AND PRINCIPALITIES IN MUSIC

With rock music being popular from generation to generation, we have gone from playing records backward in the 1970s in order to reveal satanic influence to openly offering up satanic lyrics today. I recall as a young teen, against my parents' wishes, I would save up my money to buy the latest rock album when it hit the stores. And upon my bringing it home, my uncle, who in many ways helped keep an eye on me, would inspect the lyrics inside the album cover while shaking his head in disagreement.

There are many stories of conspiracy that suggest that one must "sell their soul to the devil" to make it in the music industry. In my research on the subject, I have heard the testimony of John Todd, a former occultist and the former manager of Zodiac Productions.[4] At the time of the interview, which was in 1979, Zodiac Productions owned RCA Records, Columbia Records, Motown Records, and nearly all of the concert booking agencies in the United States. Todd, a born-again Christian, began spilling inside information as it relates to the music industry. He stated that before a new album was released, the finished master copy was taken to "the temple room" of the music company. It was then placed on an altar, and thirteen chosen witches would conjure up powers and principalities and order them to have demons under them follow every copy that was to be distributed.

Todd went on to detail the chain of command, stating that record companies were owned by bigger companies, which were ultimately all owned by the Rothschilds. He described a ranking system of witches across the country that had been set up by funds from the Rothschilds, with the state of California having the most witchcraft activities in the entire world. These witches, he said, consider the Rothschilds to be living gods, the sons and daughters of Lucifer.

I suppose that in light of such information, we can understand why music is so powerful and influential. It may also shed light on this verse: "The sound of harpists, musicians, flutists, and trumpeters shall not be heard in you anymore" (Rev. 18:22, NKJV).

Many musicians over the years have come out and admitted to the press that they gave up their souls in a contract with the "chief in command, who rules the unseen world." Most notable is Bob Dylan, who confessed this in an interview with *60 Minutes*.[5] Furthermore, many icons in the music industry have come to early deaths by drug overdose—so many that I will not list them here, but the first one was Elvis Presley, who is considered the first icon of rock 'n' roll music. Could it be that trading their eternal soul for fame and fortune turned out to be simply not worth it? Did they lose all hope and give in to suicide?

In the late 1980s, we saw the birth of a new music genre known as rap and hip-hop. Its history can be studied the same as rock 'n' roll, and it has the same conclusions—a subtle, rebellious beginning, leading to an even worse outcome than rock music. With constant profanity and racial slurs, plus the constant promotion of murder, drug use, and prostitution, rap and hip-hop have cost more lives and souls than rock—and in a shorter space of time, at that.

We can certainly expect that the terms of agreement and contracts are the same in the rap genre as they are with rock music. Possibly the most recognized icon in the history of rap music, Tupac Shakur, even spoke about the Illuminati "elite ones" who exchanged souls for fame. On

September 13, 1996, Shakur was murdered in California, and to this day, his killer has not been brought to justice. This has fueled some to believe that the Illuminati had him killed.[6] The same has been suggested about the king of pop, Michael Jackson, who also spoke of Illuminati conspiracies shortly before his death from a drug overdose on June 25, 2009.[7]

While we cannot prove or disprove that demonic forces are mingled into our music at the command of the world elite, we certainly know these genres of music have had a very negative effect on our lives. As I have said, I myself was a fan of the music, until I woke up and realized something more was behind it.

THE MULTI-BILLION-DOLLAR PORN INDUSTRY

With pornographic film companies pumping out millions of films from California and porn sites streaming online, pornography has been viewed worldwide in many nations. Never before in human history could someone, at the touch of a button, become engaged in an act of fornication with total strangers from various places in the world.

> "The kings of the earth who committed fornication and lived luxuriously with her will weep and lament for her, when they see the smoke of her burning."
>
> —REVELATION 18:9, NKJV

> "For true and righteous are His judgments, because He has judged the great harlot who corrupted the earth with her fornication."
>
> —REVELATION 19:2, NKJV

Can we now clearly discern this prophecy as technology has allowed such things to be possible? I believe so. Here are some facts about pornography that may surprise and disgust you, as they did me. As of 2010, there were more than 4.2 million porn sites on the Internet (12 percent of all websites), 68 million daily pornographic search engine requests (25 percent of all search engine requests), and 2.5 billion e-mails exchanged daily with pornographic images (8 percent of all e-mails).[8] Plus, 40 million Americans say they view pornography on a regular basis.[9]

A survey among young Christian adults has revealed that 29 percent of born-again Christians believe it is acceptable to view movies with explicit sexual content.[10] Today, even mobile phones are streaming pornography, accounting for more than $2 billion of the total $15 billion the industry takes in annually.[11] Let's imagine for a moment how much better the world we live in would be if we put that kind of money into offering plates and charities. Many people rob God by not paying tithes or giving offerings, and then look at what they do with His money!

If there truly are Christians out there who believe it is acceptable to view sexually explicit material, then we need to clean the house of God and wake them up. Jesus will not live in sin, so if you think that you have Him near, He has excused Himself and left your presence as you watch that sort of material. I challenge anyone who doubts me on this to pray about it and ask the Lord sincerely to reveal His truth to them.

I also encourage everyone who reads this to reach out to someone you know who is lost and needs directions to the Lord Jesus Christ. Changing our lives can often start with a few simple words from someone. It can be as simple as not politely laughing at a co-worker's crude jokes. Now, what happens because of that is that he will think twice about telling the joke to the next person. Therefore, you will have spared many others from hearing it without even saying a word.

Babies Murdered by the Millions

If there is one sin that puts the nail in our coffin, that has without a doubt made God furious, it is abortion—the cold-blooded murder of innocent, unborn children. Did you know the most dangerous place in the world to be today is the womb? More than 1 million babies are aborted in this nation every year. It is estimated that 98 percent of those abortions are for non-medical reasons.[12]

Abortion was legalized in the US in 1973 with *Roe v. Wade*. Allow me to describe the process of this act that happens every twenty seconds in our nation.

- *Suction abortion:* Used during the first three months of pregnancy. A suction tube is inserted into the womb, and the limbs of the baby are torn off. Eventually, the whole body is sucked out.

- *Dilation and curettage:* Used after the third month of the pregnancy. The cervix is dilated, ring forceps are inserted into the womb, and the baby is extracted piece by piece.

- *Dilation and extraction:* Used after thirteen weeks of pregnancy. The cervix is dilated, and the baby is dismembered with pliers, like forceps. Force is needed to pull the baby apart. The instrument is used to seize a leg

or other body part and then, with a twisting
motion, to tear it from the baby's body.
The baby's spine is snapped and the skull
crushed. After the baby parts are removed,
they are reassembled on a tray to make sure
they are all out.

To spare you further disgust, I have not included the
cruel procedure of partial-birth abortion. But as you can
imagine, it is nothing short of what a soulless monster,
right out of a horror film, would do to a child.

Now, if this has made you sick, imagine how God
must feel after more than forty years of being witness
to its legality! There must be a strong remnant of God's
people praying for this country for it to still be inhabitable,
because this act is absolutely vile. And with the majority
of abortions being conducted due to social/economic reasons, it is an absolute abomination. If people would only
trust in God, they would not go hungry, nor would their
children they aborted.

Even worse than the worries of finances having to do
with feeding another mouth, the most likely reason is
that they don't want to spend less money on themselves.
Having a baby doesn't fit their lifestyle or agenda.

They shouldn't be having sex! Think of it this way: You
certainly wouldn't be willing to kill someone just to have
sex. Yet you have sex knowing there is a chance you could
conceive someone and that if that happens, you will just
kill the baby before it is born. But Jesus said: "See that
you do not despise one of these little ones, for I say to you
that their angels in heaven continually see the face of My
Father who is in heaven" (Matt. 18:10, NAS).

In my study of the Bible, and having read religious

books such as the Apocrypha and the Quran, I have found interesting similarities in these readings regarding the last days, all of which give strange revelations. Let's take a look at prophecies concerning women who are pregnant in the last days:

> "And woe unto them that are with child, and to them that give suck in those days!"
>
> —MATTHEW 24:19

> There shall be chaos also in many places, and fire shall often break out, and the wild beasts shall roam beyond their haunts, and menstruous women shall bring forth monsters.
>
> —2 ESDRAS 5:8

> The day when you will see that every nursing mother will forget her suckling baby, and every pregnant female will drop her unformed load.
>
> —SURAH 22.2

Could it be that God, in the last days, has had enough of abortion? And stopped delivering souls into the womb of pregnant women, therefore creating a soulless monster to be born or causing the abortion to take place of its own accord ("dropping unformed loads")? Many debate whether or not an unborn child is considered a living being with a soul, and at what stage of the pregnancy the child is considered to be so. As with all things, the Word of God will clarify this for us: "Before I formed you in the womb I knew you, and before you were born I consecrated you; I have appointed you a prophet to the nations" (Jer. 1:5, NAS).

Let us not forget that the most obvious sign that this

is undeniably a sin is in the Ten Commandments: "Thou shalt not kill" (Exod. 20:13). And yet every twenty seconds that pass, we kill another baby and would-be prophet of God. Therefore, we have become drunk with the blood of the saints, who were without fault or sin, for one is born in sin, and they were not given birth: "I saw the woman, drunk with the blood of the saints and with the blood of the martyrs of Jesus. And when I saw her, I marveled with great amazement" (Rev. 17:6, NKJV).

There is no doubt: We are on the road to the wrath of God. As the nation is confidently traveling along, sure of its destination, we as Christians must wave down the lost and give them a road map with proper directions. And much like the advancement of technology, which increases the speed at which we can travel, we have witnessed the advancement of our nation's sins, therefore burying the needle in the speedometer, even while traveling down a dead end road.

In the days of the Bible, there was much fasting and praying to show devotion to God, as well as to receive answers and revelations. Fasting commonly consisted of shunning food and not eating for a period of time, in order to avoid the pleasures of the world. Today, we have many distractions and pleasures that we can avoid for set periods of time that would be considered a form of fasting that wouldn't even leave us hungry. For example, if our ears are constantly open to music and entertainment, we have closed the window of conversation with God. And how can we receive a word from God if we are not listening? Jesus said: "It is written, Man shall not live by bread alone, but by every word that proceedeth out of the mouth of God" (Matt. 4:4).

Chapter 3

TRENDS AND THE SINNERS
WHO SET THEM

IN AMERICA, MANY new trends come and go, but some seem to stick with us forever. Set by few and eventually followed by the masses, sheeplike people everywhere blend together, doing the same exact things. If you had the chance to peer into the future, let's say back in the mid-'90s, to see what one great new thing everyone around every corner had today, would you have scratched your head in confusion to see that is was simply a phone?

And with so many people seemingly hypnotized, with their faces constantly drawn to that tiny screen, absorbing media and text gossip, one must wonder how they are so out of touch with current events. I suppose the statistics are accurate—there really are that many people wasting their time viewing porn and playing video games!

A topic that is brought up often among Christian people but barely debated is the trend of wearing tattoos. I can speak freely on this subject, having tattoos myself. Many

Christians feel that it is a sin, while some say it may be wrong, but they do it anyway, as they are simply not sure. Tattoos, once only found on soldiers returning home from war and on motorcycle gangs, were soon found on music idols, athletes, and celebrities of all kinds. And today, following the trends of our idols, the masses have become tatted out.

Let's break it down like this. Common sense tells us that if something hurts us, don't do it. If it causes pain or harm to our body, then it is not meant to be. Another little clue to the answer is a statement that many people with multiple tattoos often say: "It's so addictive." Addiction is a common anthem in the sins that we commit. I have learned over the years that every time I do something I shouldn't, or find myself somewhere I shouldn't be, God gives me a little nudge. He lets me know He does not approve. And nearly every tattoo session I had, I see now that I was ignoring the nudge.

So, is it a sin to get a tattoo? With the knowledge of my research and ultimately my answer from God, yes it is. Will you go to hell because you have tattoos? Not if you have repented and asked forgiveness, as is the case with any other sin.

With the original purpose of a tattoo being of personal importance and deep meaning, people today will tattoo anything and everything on themselves just to cover their skin. I have seen it all—tattoos of cartoon characters, hot dogs and hamburgers, furniture, and even kitchenware.

Allow me to continue making my case, as I do my best to convince you and hopefully give you a sound opinion, if and when this subject comes up with someone you know. Tattoos are ultimately a form of bondage, just like the bondage of alcoholism, drug abuse, and pornography.

The devil hates God, and we were created in God's image, yet through all these things, the devil changes our image. Little by little, the more you give in to demonic influence, the more power the demons have over you. Like the old saying, "A marijuana cigarette leads to cocaine, and the cocaine leads you to something even stronger." Eventually you find yourself half-dead, highly dependent on expensive habits that a demon has convinced you that you cannot live without.

Let's take a look at the Scriptures concerning these things. The first verse I consider to be a real eye-opener, linking demon possession with tattooing, compulsive cutting, or self-harm:

> And always, night and day, he was in the mountains, and in the tombs, crying, and cutting himself with stones.
>
> —MARK 5:5

> Ye shall not make any cuttings in your flesh for the dead, nor print any marks upon you: I am the LORD.
>
> —LEVITICUS 19:28

Thankfully, the Bible tells us that we will receive a new body and be translated to incorruptibility. Many ask themselves, *If I have already tattooed myself, what's it gonna hurt to get another?* Well, if you are convinced that it is a sin, then you are sinning again—just like the addict who continues to use drugs. And secondly, it's going to hurt you! Recall the process of the needles stabbing into your skin? And now your tattoos are adding up and the sin has become iniquity. We all know we should not sin and shrug it off, just because we can continue to ask for forgiveness.

A LUST FOR BLOOD, GUTS, AND HORROR

In the realm of entertainment, we have seen the progressive trend toward violence, gore, sorcery, and horror. Films that terrified former generations are laughed at today. While we know that there is a "spirit of fear" and that it is not of God, we have taken much pleasure over the years in being frightened—with some obvious side effects, such as nightmares and looking over our shoulders when nothing is there.

While all forms of entertainment direct our attention away from God, some route our attention directly to the devil. There is no doubt that some films have a heavier influence than others. When being viewed in your home, you can actually feel that they change the atmosphere, even from another room, and even if you aren't viewing the film yourself.

One such film is *The Exorcist*. Released in 1973, it earned ten Academy Award nominations and grossed more than $441 million worldwide. In the film, a young girl is depicted as having been possessed by demons and then exorcised by two priests. The creator of the story based the film on actual events that took place decades earlier.

The Exorcist has been dubbed by many to be a "cursed movie" for various reasons. Due to a studio fire, important sets had to be reconstructed before production. The film's creator stated that due to odd occurrences, they had a priest bless the set. During a scene that involved the thrashing around of actress Linda Blair, a vital harness snapped, causing permanent damage to her spine. It has been said by several cast and crew members that many personal injuries were sustained during the production of the film, and a total of nine people directly and indirectly involved with the film came to untimely deaths.[1]

Many horror films throughout the years have obtained cult status with huge fan bases, with characters becoming idols to the fans, such as Dracula, Frankenstein, Freddy Krueger, and others. This could create a very nightmarish reality for the world someday if we consider God's judgment of idol worship, as it is described in the Apocrypha:

> In return for their foolish and wicked thoughts, which led them astray to worship irrational serpents and worthless animals, thou didst send upon them a multitude of irrational creatures to punish them, that they might learn that one is punished by the very things by which he sins....Not only could their damage exterminate men, but the mere sight of them could kill by fright.
>
> —WISDOM OF SOLOMON 11:15–16, 19

So, could we one day see creatures that were thought to only exist in horror films appear on the earth as a punishment for idolizing demonic creatures, monsters, and maniacal killers? I suppose the punishment would fit the crime.

THOSE AREN'T ALIENS—THEY'RE DEMONS

Another trend in film has been the aliens-from-outer-space theme. While Americans and people worldwide increasingly continue to capture and catalogue unexplainable images in the sky, Hollywood has pushed an agenda to help deceive the masses. While there have been count-less films about destructive alien invasions, there have also been many that portray aliens as harmless beings who can help us and teach us how to live a more efficient life.

But an increasing amount of people, along with myself, are coming to the theory that if beings are really visiting us, they are "demons in alien clothing." Having come to this conclusion a few years ago, I have been waiting to see if Hollywood would touch on this theory—and in 2011, with the release of the movie *Paul*, they certainly did.

In the film, two friends from Europe travel to America for a comic book convention and go sightseeing in their RV, visiting places that were known for historical extra-terrestrial activities. Along the way, a small, friendly alien escapes from a secret base and hitches a ride with them. They also pick up a young woman from a country setting who lived with her father. It is made obvious that she is a Christian, and the jokes about her religion begin and con-tinue throughout the entire film. The woman points out that the alien is likely a demon, and she is quickly dubbed a flat-earth theorist and re-educated by the other charac-ters. In no time at all, she proclaims how wonderful it is to become informed and to let go of an old, oppressive religion.

Having a personal interest in the subject of unidenti-fied flying objects and stories of alien encounters, I have reviewed thousands of photos, videos, and eyewitness tes-timonies involving them. Possibly the most compelling evidence I have found is in the presentation and testimony of a man named Phil Schneider,[2] also known as the man who killed two alien Greys.

Schneider's description of alien beings who live in cav-erns beneath the earth is worth considering if we identify them as demons. And with more than seventeen years of experience in government black projects, Schneider had much to tell. Working as a biologist and structural engineer for the government, his job was to oversee the development and construction of deep underground military bases. He stated that in 1995, at the time of the interview, more than 130 of these bases existed in the US and more than 1400 existed worldwide. Schneider estimated that each one cost $17 billion to construct and that the funds to build them came out of the annual black project budget, which is twice as large as the annual military budget. Schneider spoke of Groom Lake, S2, S4, Area 51, and many other top-secret bases.

Schneider's story is this. In 1979, when beginning the construction of one of these bases in Dulce, New Mexico, Schneider and his group came across a group of alien beings inside caverns deep in the earth. A firefight took the lives of several government agents and army personnel. Schneider killed two of the beings, and in the process they shot him with some kind of laser flash weapon, which cut off three of his fingers and also gave him cancerous tumors. He claimed the government had an agreement with these beings for many decades and that in exchange for technological advancement, we allow them to conduct horrific genetic experiments on abducted human beings in the lowest levels of the bases, which is known as "Nightmare Hall."

Less than one year after giving these lectures, which were filmed by audience members, Schneider was found dead, apparently strangled with a piano wire. What was extremely convincing to me about Schneider's testimony was the technology he spoke about. The lecture was recorded in 1995, during which he described a Mach-2

Maglev train system that connected all the underground bases. Just in the past few years, we have heard of and seen these trains in Japan. They travel along on a magnetic railway, actually hovering above it, thus giving them their name, *maglev*, which is short for "magnetic levitation."

Ultimately, Schneider's goal was to inform the public that a very dark time is coming and that there is a global government plan involving these beings to kill off much of the population and enslave those who remain. He said the goal for this plan was to be reached by the year 2020 or no later than 2025.

If we consider these beings to be demonic entities rather than beings from outer space, it is not that far-fetched an idea, especially considering that there are demonic forces at work behind government priorities, such as unarming the population and implanting microchips, which is discussed in the healthcare bill that was recently passed.

If you are interested in the subject, I recommend you watch Schneider's lecture, as I have barely scratched the surface of his evidence. You can find the lecture on YouTube, along with many others telling similar tales of days working for the government black projects.

Whether we talk about film, music, or even the clothes we wear, there is something behind everything. When you buy a new shirt or pair of pants, you have subconsciously made moral decisions that led you to buy them. Maybe you passed up that t-shirt with questionable images or script on it or a skirt that was made to be too short. Though they might have looked good on you, and you even received a thumbs-up from a friend, you passed the moral test.

I believe in the case of many Christian people today, they have not only ignored their better judgment, but they have totally turned off the switch. We increasingly seem to be doing whatever we want. If it makes me feel good, I do it, goes the reasoning, and God would want me to feel good. If the new comedy film I rent and watch makes me laugh, even though it has much profanity, it's fine; God would want me to laugh and be happy.

This is the downward spiral. Little by little, we sin, and we don't even notice we are falling away until we have problems and unanswered prayers. If you continue to sin and expect God to have your back in the bad times, He will remember having only seen your back in the good times, because you turned your back on Him! Let's stop fooling ourselves. We must strive each day to become closer to the Lord and to live in holiness. We face a major war with all the sins that are taking place in our nation. We cannot go on living with one foot in the church and one foot in the world. If we cannot convince the sinner to avoid the sin and the lost to be saved, at least we will know that we put forth our best effort—and we cannot do so unless we project a sinless example.

The trend of modern Christians being more open to opinion of what is right or wrong is one that I feel is of great importance. It starts with something small, such as it being considered acceptable by the majority of the congregation to watch films with questionable content. And then a small group of members decides it is acceptable to drink alcohol on a regular basis. And then another small group of members decides it is acceptable to be a gay Christian—because God loves everybody, right?

And then one day, among these small groups that hold different opinions, someone will rebuke one of the members who believes in gay marriage, and they in turn will point their finger at the alcoholics, and so on. Meanwhile, the devil is looking in the window, laughing and saying, "These are your people, God! What a joke!"

We must take action before it comes to this type of scenario. If sin is in the church, stand up against it. Speak loudly if you must. Jesus Christ Himself went into a fit of rage, turning over tables as He rebuked the moneychangers because they had defiled the temple.

If we get ourselves into the practice of keeping God on our minds throughout the day, we are less likely to sin. For if we are tempted at any point in the day, the temptation will be easily recognized for what it is, having had God fresh in our thoughts.

Consider all the false religions and false gods of this world and how their followers devote themselves every day to their beliefs, some praying even five times a day with their heads bowed down on the earth. They fast and stand firm in their faith in a god who isn't genuine. Surely, if they can devote such worship and prayer to a false god, we can be equally devoted, if not more, to the one true God! Think about it—even those we consider worshippers of false gods shun and protest the indecent material that today's Christians partake of!

Chapter 4

ISLAM IN AMERICA

I N THE YEAR AD 610, at age forty, the self-proclaimed
prophet Muhammad created the religion of Islam. The
meaning of *Islam* is translated as "the submission to
the will of God." And the meaning of *Muslim* is translated
as "one who submits." Having founded one of the three
monotheistic religions, Muhammad began preaching to
the people of Mecca that they should abandon their poly-
theistic beliefs.

In the beginning, he claimed to have been visited by
Gabriel, the angel, who gave him revelations from God
while he was living in a cave. Soon after, he began sharing
the news of the angel's revelations. He wasn't received well
or considered a true prophet, and Jews and Christians dis-
missed his claims. After this, Muhammad became bitter
toward them, claiming his God is the same God of the
Jews and Christians—the God of Abraham. Yet Muslims
call their God *Allah*, which is a name that actually pre-
dates Islam as the name of a moon diety.

It is said that Muhammad had seizures at times when he was in the cave. I personally believe he was visited by a demon, or perhaps Satan himself, as the Bible tells us that even Satan can appear as an angel of light.

Having not been accepted by Jews or Christians, Muhammad began to speak out against them, teaching his growing number of followers that they were infidels. While he recognized that Jesus was born of the virgin Mary and was a prophet, Muhammad claimed that Jesus was not the son of God and that He was not actually crucified. He also stated that God was not begat, nor did He beget, and that anyone who believed in the Trinity would surely burn in hell.

Muhammad told his followers that he was to correct the corrupted Scriptures, which were the Torah and the Gospels. After his death, in AD 632, his writings and the memories of his teachings were compiled into a book, known today as the Quran and considered by Muslims to be their holy book.

Muhammad's successor, Abu Bakr, who was his close friend and father-in-law, was elected by one of Muhammad's close companions as the first caliphate. Soon after Abu Bakr became the caliphate, there was civil war, which led the religion to split into two tribes, the Sunni and the Shia. The majority of Muslims today are Sunni, making up about 80 percent. To this day, the two tribes still fight and kill one another over disputes, such as which tribe will produce their awaited one, the Mahdi, whom many Christians now believe will be the Antichrist of the Bible.

At the time of Muhammad's death, it is estimated that there were as many as a few hundred followers of Muhammad. Being considered the second largest religion in the world today, with Christianity being the largest,

Islam is the fastest-growing religion in the world. With an estimated 1.62 billion Muslims worldwide, making up more than 20 percent of the world's population.[1] This is due to the fact that they believe in forced conversion and is also a result of the men having multiple wives who each bear many children.

The ultimate goal of Islam is to conquer the world—to convert the infidels even if by force or to behead those who will not believe. Having made world news in recent years, many Muslim immigrants have come to Europe and are now causing cultural clashes and protests regarding European law. They wish to establish sharia law, the law of Islam, as the global, one-world law. With churches and properties being bought and converted to mosques and Islamic centers, Muslims have been successful in spreading their religion through infiltration rather than invasion.

If a Muslim tells you Islam is a religion of peace, it is like a Christian telling you they do not subscribe to the majority of Scriptures in the Bible. The Quran speaks of such Muslims who would consider it a peaceful religion:

> War is prescribed for you, even though you dislike war. But you may dislike a thing that is good for you and that you may love a thing that is bad for you.
>
> —SURAH 2.216

> Fight them, Allah will punish them by your hands and bring them to disgrace.
>
> —SURAH 9.14

> Be not weary and faint hearted, crying for peace, for you have the upper hand with Allah.
>
> —SURAH 47.35

So many moderate Muslims living peaceful lives obviously disregard such teachings that are found in their holy book, the Quran. But what is to say that one day they won't have a leap of faith, triggered by some world event or future prophet who makes them all follow the teachings word for word? I believe it is a very likely scenario that will someday occur. And in that event, moderate Muslims in every part of the world will stand beside even the most extreme Muslims in the fight and slaughter for Allah.

Let's take a look at some of the teachings from the Quran that could inspire even the most moderate Muslim to engage in acts of terror:

> I will cast terror into the hearts of those who disbelieve. Therefore, strike off their heads and strike off every fingertip of them.
>
> —SURAH 8.12

> The punishment of those who wage war against Allah and his prophet is only this, that they should be murdered or crucified or their hands and feet should be cut off.
>
> —SURAH 5.33

> Therefore when you meet the unbelievers in battle, strike hard at their necks until you have completely defeated them.
>
> —SURAH 47.4

And from the Hadith, we read:

> The hour will not be established until you fight with the Jews, and the stone behind which a Jew

will be hiding will say; "O Muslim! There is a Jew hiding behind me, so kill him."

—BUKHARI 52:177

While these are just a few examples of justifiable violent actions, the theme is the same throughout the entire Quran. So, how did we become a nation that has an estimated 2.5 million Muslims in it, when their history and ideology is so different than ours? Let's take a look at the history of Islamic movements in America and see if we can pinpoint its arrival and why it has become widely accepted.

In the colonial days of America, many of the slaves brought from Africa were of the Muslim faith. By the year 1800, there were an estimated 500,000 Africans in America. Historians estimate that between 15 to 30 percent of all enslaved African men were Muslims. From the 1880s to 1914, thousands of Muslims immigrated to America from the Ottoman Empire and also parts of South Asia.[2] The Muslim population began to rapidly grow through immigration and conversion, but mostly due to a very high birth rate.

After many African American men and women were converted to Christianity, many more immigrants came to America who had no desire to abandon their Islamic beliefs. In the early 1900s, mosques began to be constructed around the country, one of the first being in the state of Maine, established by Albanian immigrants in 1915. Today, it is estimated that there are more than 1200 mosques nationwide.

In 1913, a small group of African American citizens formed a group called the Moorish Science Temple of America. It was based on Islamic and black supremacy teachings. Its founder, Timothy Drew, taught that black people were of Moorish origin and descendants of the Moabites and that they had lost their Muslim identity through slavery. The group also took inspiration from Buddhism, Christianity, Freemasonry, gnosticism, and Taoism. In the 1930s, membership had grown to more than 30,000 people, with one-third of its members residing in Chicago.[3]

In July 1930, the Nation of Islam was founded by Wallace D. Fard Muhammad in Detroit, Michigan. Its stated goals were to improve the spiritual, mental, social, and economic condition for African Americans and all of humanity. Critics of the religious movement have viewed it as being black supremacist and anti-Semitic. Its headquarters are located in Chicago. Some of Fard's followers believed he was the Messiah of Christianity and the Mahdi of Islam.[4]

Within its first year, the Nation of Islam had already attracted more than 25,000 members. Reaching out to African Americans, the group said it was foolish for black people to be Christians, as they considered it a white man's religion. During World War II, they advised their members and all African Americans to avoid the draft, because, they said, America had never done anything to help black people and it was a white man's war. The group also teaches that God is black, as was the first created man, Adam.

Not that the color of God or Adam much matter, but I have found no evidence to support that theory. In fact, I have only found evidence against it. In my study of the works of Flavius Josephus, the Jewish historian, he speaks of the first created man, Adam, whose name in Hebrew signifies "one that is red in color." God called him Adam, and he was formed by God out of the red earth.

While in prison for robbery from 1946–1952, Malcolm Little joined the Nation of Islam.[5] Influenced by his brother, Reginald, who had become a member in Detroit, he quickly rose to the top and became the national representative of the Nation of Islam and replaced his surname with an *X*, which was a custom of followers, for they believed their surnames were imposed on them by white slaveholders. Malcolm X eventually left the Nation of Islam and founded Muslim Mosque, Inc.

When Malcolm X departed the Nation of Islam in 1964, he was replaced by Louis Farrakhan,[6] formerly known as Louis X and originally known as Louis Walcott. To this day, he remains the leader of the Nation of Islam.

Having briefly covered the history of the Nation of Islam, let's take a look at some of their beliefs that make them unique. First, they believe their founder, Wallace D. Fard, was God incarnate. They teach that the Earth and moon were once the same and that the Earth is more than 76 trillion years old. They teach that Hitler was a great man and that Jews have been responsible for orchestrating an African American holocaust. Farrakhan states that they have done this by being the slum lords of African American communities and that they are the wicked promoters of the filth that comes from Hollywood, encouraging homosexuality and lesbianism.

Its adherents also have a wide variety of conspiracy theories, one of which suggests the American government created the events of September 11, 2001, for the sole purpose of gaining oil-rich territories in Afghanistan.

It is known that there are many groups in the United States that have been funding terrorist organizations, such as Hamas, and it is estimated that there may be as many as 800 sleeper cells waiting for the green light to engage in acts of terror on the American people. One such group is the Muslim Brotherhood.

In a trial involving a group that funded terrorist organizations, a memorandum on the strategic goals of such groups entered into evidence. It stated that their work, and the work of many similar groups in America, was like a grand *jihad* (holy war) to eliminate and destroy Western civilization from within and ultimately sabotage what they call "the miserable nation" so that Islam could be made victorious over all other religions. While many have been convicted of supporting terror groups, there are many more that are still active to this day.

While there are very different beliefs between the Nation of Islam and Islam itself, neither one can be viewed as a positive religious belief system for America. As we can see when looking at the history of the Nation of Islam, many are drawn in simply because of racial factors. Conversely, we know that Christianity is a color-blind faith. Anyone of any ethnic background is accepted. Would you leave heaven if, upon your arrival, you discovered God to be a different color than you had previously imagined? Certainly not. So why, then, would you choose a religion based on racial factors?

We know that Jesus Christ never owned slaves, and yet Muhammad did. We know that Jesus Christ lived a sinless life as an example to mankind, and we know that Muhammad did not. There are many reasons for one to choose Christianity over Islam if a person find him or herself in search of the truth. And we must help people like this do so, for there are many out there only too willing to lead them down the wrong path.

Let's review a few of the major inconsistencies and contradictions that I have discovered in the Quran, which should only further convince someone to reconsider their Islamic beliefs, for we know God would not be mistaken or confused, and neither would a true prophet who was destined to interpret His truth.

CONTRADICTIONS REGARDING CREATION

It is He who created man from water.

—SURAH 25.54

In the name of thy Lord and cherisher, who created man, out of a mere clot of blood.

—SURAH 96.1–2

We created man from sounding clay, from mud molded into shape.

—SURAH 15.26

INCONSISTENCIES REGARDING THE FIRST MUSLIM

He has no partners: This am I commanded, and I am the first of those who bow to his will.

—SURAH 6.163

And Musa [Moses] fell down being unconscious. When he came back to his senses he said: "Glory be to you! To you I come in repentance, and I am the first one to believe."

—SURAH 7.143

41

HISTORICAL INCONSISTENCIES REGARDING THE BIRTH OF JESUS

In several Suras the quran confuses the virgin Mary (*Miriam* in Hebrew) with Miriam, the sister of Aaron and Moses. There were 1400 years between the two women.

> At length she brought the babe to her people, carrying Him in her arms, they said, "O Mary! Truly a strange thing has thou brought! O sister of Aaron, thy father was not a man of evil, nor your mother a woman unchaste!"
>
> —SURAH 19.27–28

CONTRADICTIONS CONCERNING MURDER

> Do not kill your children on an excuse of want, do not take life, which Allah has made sacred, except by justice and law.
>
> —SURAH 6.151

> And slay them wherever ye find them, for the persecution of Muslims is worse than the slaughter of non believers.
>
> —SURA 2.191

Many people believe the God of the Bible is the same God known as Allah in the Quran. Muslims insist this to be factual, as Muhammad stated that his duty was to correct the Torah (the five books of Moses) and the Gospels. But there are countless differences between the God of the Bible and Allah. Allah in the Quran is unknowable, whereas the God of the Bible is knowable. Allah is impersonable, unlike the personal God the Scriptures reveal.

Allah is Unitarian, where the God we know is Trinitarian. And so on and so forth.

The best evidence to make the case that Islam is a false religion is probably the fact that it did not surface until more than six hundred years after the life of Jesus Christ. Therefore, it would be quite simple to create a new religion, with twisted and different versions of the former. If God truly needed the Scriptures to be corrected, assuming Jesus was not the Son of God, He would not have waited six hundred years to do so. Another telling sign is that Muhammad initially feared that he was possessed by the being that came to him inside the cave, whereas prophets of the Bible immediately identified that they were encountering—and speaking on behalf of—the Spirit of God.

Another interesting sign is that Muhammad claimed it was his goal as a prophet to correct the Scriptures, yet the Quran is mostly made up of the memories of those who heard Muhammad speak, not his actual writings. It is also interesting that Muslims face Mecca when praying, which is in the region of the world where Satan first convinced man to sin and is considered by many to be the devil's atmosphere. Last but not least, Jesus Himself warned us that false prophets and false Christs would appear. Muhammad fulfilled this prophetic word of Jesus, without even realizing it!

History was made in 2008, with the election of the first African American president, Barack Hussein Obama. Before he was even elected, many questions were raised concerning his religious background. We knew that his father, Barack Sr., was a Muslim from Kenya and that his mother, Ann, was an atheist from Kansas. The prospects of his religious foundation did not look good, to say the least. His father believed in what we consider to be a false religion, and his mother believed in...well, nothing.

It was soon made clear, however, that Barack Obama was, in fact, a Christian. He and his family attended Trinity United Church of Christ in Chicago. However, excerpts of sermons taught by the pastor, Jeremiah Wright,[7] soon made headline news and sparked much debate. In some of the sermons, the pastor gave the strong impression that the church was anti-Semitic and that America was a terror state. Recounting the events of World War II, Wright said we bombed Hiroshima and Nagasaki and therefore deserved the terror attacks of 9/11. Wright also proclaimed the nation was racist toward African Americans, referring to the nation as the United States of the KKK. He even went so far to say, from the pulpit, that God should damn America. It also came out that he was close personal friends with Louis Farrakhan, the leader of the Nation of Islam, and had been for more than thirty years. He was accused of anti-Semitism when stating, "The Zionist Jews are conducting genocide on the Palestinians in Gaza."

Whether or not Barack Obama is in favor of the Islamic religion, there is no question he is the first president to be elected with such ties and associations with it. It is also historical that he was the first president who was elected because of his skin color, with many African American voters and white voters alike confessing they voted for him because he was black.

Many people believed this would send a message to the world, that Americans weren't all white Christian conservatives who would dare to invade Muslim countries. And in so many ways, I suppose it did. There have been many instances where President Obama proclaimed us to be good friends of Muslim countries. He proclaimed during his campaign that America is not a Christian nation but a nation of many diverse religions.

He also became increasingly apologetic to the nations of the world. He was seen on television by many bowing to the Saudi king. And yet, not once in his first term as president did he visit the land of Israel. President Obama is viewed by many to be the least friendly president to the nation of Israel in American history. This should come as no surprise, though, considering the anti-Semitic views of his church. And as a result of his apologetic approach, we are now taken less seriously and seen as being less likely to engage in a war.

In December 2011, a highly sensitive US stealth drone conducting surveillance in Afghanistan went off-course and was recovered by Iran. When we confirmed this to be true, President Obama called on the Iranian government to return our property. As you can imagine, they basically laughed in our face—and not only that, but they warned of severe consequences in the event of its happening again.

While I am happy to say that I live in a country that provides freedom of religion, since freedom of will was given to us by God, it is still upsetting that so many Americans have chosen Islam over Christianity. This could be because of the fact that so many Christians in America today project a sinful way of life. We must first get our priorities straight within our own beliefs before we can effectively direct our fellow citizens to the Lord Jesus Christ.

I'm sure that many of you have identified Islam as an exact opposite of the Christian faith, through just the few examples given in this chapter. I feel that while it is most important to study the Scriptures of the Holy Bible, it is also to our advantage to be aware of other beliefs. In the event of a debate with a non-Christian, we may find them telling us they worship the same God we do, but our prior knowledge of their beliefs can help us not only deny this claim but also explain to them why.

Many people strive to gain admiration and the praise of men on earth, and some work tirelessly to achieve awards that can be displayed in a proud fashion. But after all their virtues and recognition have brought them praise and reward, what more can they look forward to when the concerns of this life have expired?

Much happier is the one who has worked tirelessly to win souls for the kingdom of heaven, fed the poor when they were hungry, or clothed the needy when they were naked. This man goes to his grave unrewarded, unknown, and counted among the failures of this world. But when he is awoken and his accomplishments proclaimed, low will be the man who gained riches, and glory in his pursuits of the former life and high will be the one who served God, even in obscurity.

Chapter 5

EARTHQUAKES AND SUPERCELLS

A s the Bible foretells, there will be an increase in earthquakes and disasters as we approach the time of the end—and there is nothing like a natural disaster to give us a wake-up call, like a loud alarm clock echoing a horrible tone throughout the house. Sadly, most people are not fully awoken by it. We hit the snooze button and go back to sleep, causing it to happen over and over again. And much like a restless person who wakes up at ten minutes till, knowing the alarm is set for the top of the hour, we disregard the signs of prophecy and go back to sleep.

Jesus said, when describing the signs of the end, that we should be sober and watch. Therefore, we should only assume that we will be able to identify the times of which he spoke—as long as we are paying close attention.

> "When you see these things happening, know that the kingdom of God is near."
>
> —Luke 21:31, nkjv

> "Watch therefore, and pray always that you may
> be counted worthy to escape all these things that
> will come to pass, and to stand before the Son of
> Man."
>
> —LUKE 21:36, NKJV

Precisely two hundred years ago, America experienced the most powerful series of earthquakes in its recorded history. Beginning on December 16, 1811, and continuing through February 1812, four great earthquakes estimated to be as high as 8.1 in magnitude, with countless aftershocks, hit our land.[1] With a pair of initial earthquakes on December 16 that occurred in northeast Arkansas, the epicenter of the following earthquakes were in New Madrid, Missouri. The events as well as the seismic zone have been named after this town.

There are estimates that the earthquakes were felt strongly over 50,000 square miles and moderately over 1 million square miles. Having epic consequences such as the destruction of homes and other man-made structures, it caused the Mississippi River to flow backward, church bells to ring in Boston, and sidewalks to crack in Washington, DC. Documented eyewitness accounts reveal a vision of horror, with some stating that there were terrible noises, like that of thunder only more hoarse and awful, and some stating that the birds of the air were screaming and that all the animals of the land were stricken with terror.

With the fault lines for these earthquakes still active today and sustaining an increasing number of small quakes, many believe there will be another series of great earthquakes comparable to those of 1811–1812. In such an event, the consequences would be far more disastrous, considering that the affected regions have since become heavily populated. According to a recent study by the University of Illinois, a 7.7-magnitude earthquake along the New Madrid fault line would leave 3,500 people dead, more than 80,000 injured, and more than 7 million homeless.[2]

Some have suggested that in the event of an earthquake greater than a magnitude 7.7, it is likely such cities as St. Louis, Missouri, and Memphis, Tennessee, would be completely destroyed. This would have a far-reaching effect on the nation, not only because of the massive need for humanitarian aid and disaster relief for those directly affected, but also because of the possibility of bridges being out of service, thus eliminating necessary routes for travel and deliveries.

We must also consider the current state of our economic crisis. In the event of such a disaster, it is likely that it would be the last straw, financially speaking, and many people would not receive the help that they would desperately need.

In just the last decade, there have been many catastrophic earthquakes in various places around the globe, with a total number of just under 700,000 fatalities. That is almost 1 million people killed by earthquakes in a span of only ten years! To name a few of the most deadly, there was the 6.6-magnitude quake in southeastern Iran on December 26, 2003, that killed 31,000 people. Then, oddly enough, one year later on December 26, 2004, there was the 9.1-magnitude quake off the west coast of Sumatra, Indonesia, that produced tsunami waves and killed nearly 230,000 people. Another major loss of life was reported as the result of the 7.0-magnitude quake in Haiti on January 12, 2010, with a death toll of 316,000.[3]

49

Many other earthquakes within the last decade have cost the lives of thousands of people. The most recent was the 9.0-magnitude quake that caused tsunami waves on March 11, 2011, in Japan, which cost the lives of more than 20,000 people. In this tragic event, Japan had to also battle the emergency of nuclear reactors melting down at the Fukushima nuclear plant, caused by the flooding from the tsunami.

I'm not sure what the connection is, if any, but looking at historical earthquakes dating as far back as the eighteenth century, the deadliest earthquakes involving more than 10,000 people almost always occurred between the months of December and April. Again, there may be no connection between these quakes and the time of year they happened, but from a biblical viewpoint, I find it interesting that this is the same timeframe that Jesus Christ was not only born, but also crucified.

Furthermore, around New Year's Day 2011, several incidents of strange phenomenon made headline news, all of which were in close proximity to the New Madrid fault. About thirty-five miles northeast of Little Rock, in Beebe, Arkansas, it was estimated that 5,000 red-winged black-birds dropped dead in mid-air and fell to the ground.[4] Within the same week, it is estimated that between 80,000 and 100,000 dead drum fish washed ashore the Arkansas river banks.[5] It was reported that the fish died due to disease and that the birds may have been killed by fireworks or sudden weather change.

This made many people suspect it was a sign of a coming disaster, such as an earthquake. It brought a substantial amount of attention to the conspiracy theories surrounding the US government program known as HAARP,[6] which is short for High Frequency Active

Auroral Research Program. Developed in 1990 and funded by the US Air Force, US Navy, the University of Alaska, and the Defense Advanced Research Projects Agency, its operations are conducted from a secure facility near Gakona, Alaska.

The official information about the HAARP program is that it exists for scientific research, regarding the potential for developing ionospheric enhancement technology for radio communications and surveillance. These studies are conducted by creating an energy from a field of powerful antennas and then injecting that energy into the ionosphere. Many respectable scientists have studied the program and come to grim conclusions. They say that not only could the actions of the program change the course of the jet stream, but also that they could have many negative effects concerning weather modification.

One of the most popular theories is that the energy created from this field, once shot into the ionosphere, could be directed back down to the earth, triggering earthquakes. Others suggest that it could be used to broadcast sounds and even spoken messages that the human ear could pick up, as well as to project images in the sky. One such theory can be found on a YouTube video that shows large blue spirals appearing in the sky. Other phenomena around the world have be reported, such as strange sounds in the atmosphere, which some have labeled trumpets and others call sky quakes.

The connection between earthquakes and HAARP has also been made from the fact that people have reported seeing strange colors in the skies, similar to the Northern Lights, across the world just prior to an earthquake. One scientist said that HAARP technology was actually inspired by Tesla's death ray and could potentially cause the sky to burn up one day. This brings to mind the Bible verse in Revelation that tells of the sky rolling up like a scroll (Rev. 6:14).

Since 2011, we have seen a sharp increase in the number of earthquakes in and around the Midwest. A recent study on the matter concluded that it could be the result of drilling into bedrock to dispose of waste water.[7] In April 2012, multiple towns in Wisconsin received reports of strange booming sounds that were heard at various times over the course of several weeks. At the time of the initial reports, seismologists declared there had been no activity, but they later stated that the noises were the result of small earthquakes that were taking place.

On August 23, 2011, a 5.8-magnitude earthquake rocked the East Coast, with its epicenter in Virginia. While there were no reports of fatalities or serious injuries, substantial damage was done to numerous structures. Large cracks were discovered at the top of the Washington Monument, large pieces of plaster fell off the Capitol building, and three pinnacles fell from the thirty-story central tower at the National Cathedral. This was the strongest earthquake to occur on the East Coast in more than sixty years.

Since early 2012, there have been many earthquakes with a magnitude of 6.0 or greater in Mexico and off the West Coast of the United States. Many fear that a strong earthquake could soon strike and trigger the eruption of Mount St. Helens volcano. In such an event, the damaging effects could be far-reaching. With volcanic ash filling our skies, it would blot out the sun and take a serious toll on our agriculture.

There is no doubt that earthquakes pose a serious threat and that they are increasing in diverse places, originating from natural occurrences, such as the shifting of plates, to man-made occurrences, such as drilling, not to mention the possibility of the Earth itself trembling in fear of the things that soon come. In the Apocrypha, when Ezra is receiving revelations from the Lord, we read the following:

> He answered and said to me, "Rise to your feet and you will hear a full, resounding voice. And if the place where you are standing is greatly shaken while the voice is speaking, do not be terrified; because the word concerns the end, and the foundations of the earth will understand that the speech concerns them. They will tremble and be shaken, for they know that their end must be changed."
>
> —2 ESDRAS 6:13

> While He spoke to me, behold, little by little the place where I was standing began to rock to and fro.
>
> —2 ESDRAS 6:29

Another natural threat that has intensified in recent years and has become more and more evident is the threat of powerful storm systems. On August 23, 2005, Hurricane Katrina formed over the Bahamas and crossed over Florida as a category 1 hurricane. By the time it reached the Gulf of Mexico and made landfall on August 29 in southeast Louisiana, it was a category 3. The storm surge caused widespread damage along the gulf coast, from central Florida to Texas.

It was the deadliest natural disaster in the history of the United States, with a confirmed death toll at 1,833, and the costliest natural disaster, with an estimated $81 billion in damages.[8]

The most affected area from the storm was the city of New Orleans. With the catastrophic failure of the federally built levee systems collapsing, more than 80 percent of the city flooded. An estimated 300,000 residents found themselves instantly homeless, and millions were without power. As the city and the areas surrounding it became the mirror image of a third-world country and many people were cut off from communication, the police were forced to focus their attention on search-and-rescue.

After the storm had wreaked its havoc and the winds subsided, the results were thousands of square miles of debris and horrific images, such as decomposing bodies that floated along flooded streets. As there were many people in shock from the sudden destruction and loss of life, society quickly broke down and fell into a lawless state. People looted stores and carried away such items as flat-screen TVs, even though there was no electricity; they took anything they could get their hands on. As a result of such loathsome and childish acts, the US military assumed police powers and initiated martial law. As many as 15,000 federal troops, national guardsmen, and private contractors from Blackwater USA began patrolling the city. Under the blanket of martial law, they began gun confiscation in a door-to-door effort. Many citizens who were only mildly affected by the storm were forced to hand over their firearms, even though it was a high probability they would need to defend themselves in the event of looters trespassing on their property.

If we have learned anything from this event, it is that chaos directly follows disaster. Society quickly breaks down and people begin to act subhuman, like mindless, hungry beasts waiting for their prey to become injured before they attack—which, in turn, creates a police state in which law-abiding citizens lose their freedoms and are left without the means to defend themselves. Ultimately, our lives then rest in the hands of the police—but what if they are too busy to come to our rescue?

In April 2011, the United States witnessed the largest-ever tornado outbreak in its recorded history.[9] Affecting the southern, midwestern, and northeastern states, it left horrific destruction in its wake. In the span of three days, between April 25 and 28, a total of 358 tornadoes were confirmed by the National Weather Service. Twenty-one states, from Texas to New York, were affected. In total, 346 people lost their lives, and the damages have been estimated at more than $11 billion.

With the violent tornadoes ripping through the states, erasing entire subdivisions and small towns, many people were left in a horrified state due to the fierce and sudden destruction. People who weren't in the direct path of the tornadoes suffered property damages from baseball-sized hail to watermelon-sized hail that was produced by the storms.

With some of the tornadoes traveling in excess of 100 miles an hour, the destruction came suddenly and the loss of life was unavoidable. Aside from the massive three-day outbreak, many other tornadoes wreaked havoc during the month of April. One such storm so extensively damaged Lambert St. Louis airport that it had to shut down operations for a short period of time to make repairs before flights could resume.

The month of May didn't prove much calmer, with the destruction of devastating tornadoes continuing to grip our attention. On May 22, 2011, a catastrophic EF5 multiple-vortex tornado struck the town of Joplin, Missouri.[10] With estimated winds at 250 miles an hour, it destroyed some two thousand buildings and seven thousand homes. An estimated 25 percent of the city was destroyed, and due to the damages incurred, it was the highest insurance payout in the history of Missouri, totaling up to $2.8 billion. The death toll was 162, and there were more than a thousand injured survivors. Many people came to their aid, proving that the compassion of fellow Americans is still very much alive.

While loss of life is most unfortunate in any event, the death tolls from these events are much lower than they could have been. This has been one indicator for me to believe such events are a warning, or a wake-up call, if you will.

With powerful storms reaching down from the sky, destroying our homes and communities, and the ground beneath us trembling as active seismic zones become hyperactive, we must not make the mistake of having a "business as usual" attitude after clean-up efforts conclude. In the event of a tragic incident, there is no better time to evaluate your life and where you stand with God. In the wake of a catastrophic event, we should first thank God for sparing our lives, and, secondly, we should show Him that we are thankful by counting our sins among the scattered debris of personal belongings no longer of use to us.

If these storms and earthquakes are truly warning signs from God, then we should certainly take some time to not only reflect on our personal lives, but also to consider future events that may occur if we do not change our ways. Let us consider the state of California, where our sinful entertainment is produced and then distributed. Its citizens have come to shrug off and even sleep through multiple earthquakes that happen every other day, going about their days with the business-as-usual mentality.

If God were to completely destroy the key areas that produce such sin and abominations, He would likely turn as many away from partaking in its sins as possible before its destruction. Going with this theory, I have to wonder if the warnings that we have received in the midwestern and surrounding states are a precursor to something catastrophic happening on the West Coast? God would most certainly want us to turn away from the sin of our own accord, rather than turning from it simply because it is no longer available.

While we must continue to shun sinful entertainment and protest as well as vote for crucial laws that concern our morality, let's not kid ourselves. Nothing short of an act of God will bring an end to it. It has become commonplace in our society, and nearly all of us support it one way or another. If we go to a theater and buy tickets for a good moral film, we are still financially supporting a theater that shows inappropriate films. And the same can be said for video stores and so many other retailers that stock inappropriate material.

Wouldn't we be proud to one day stand in front of God, knowing that we turned from sin when it was all around us? Wouldn't we be commended for such loyalty and faith? I certainly believe so. My hope is that one day, I and my family become so alien to this world that we are considered to be completely out of touch by society—to know not the things of this world, but to be completely familiar with God and His heavenly residence.

If we all strive day by day to gain knowledge from the Lord, we will begin to reap much greater rewards than that of money and earthly possessions. When we make preparations for a family vacation, do we not first learn certain things about our destination? And do we not carefully consider routes and directions on how to get there? Likewise, we must also carefully consider our eternal destination and continually follow the directions that can be found in the Bible, as well as personally keeping in touch with the Lord.

> The LORD is slow to anger, and great in power, and will not at all acquit the wicked; the LORD hath His way in the whirlwind and in the storm, and the clouds are the dust of his feet.
>
> —NAHUM 1:3

Chapter 6

GLOBAL DEPRESSION
AND WORLD WAR III

A S REPORTED BY the US National Bureau of Economic Research, the recession officially began in December 2007, with US mortgage-backed securities, which had risks that were hard to assess, being marketed around the world. A more broad-based credit boom fed the global speculative bubble in real estate and equities, which served to back the risky lending practices. The financial situation was made more difficult by a sharp increase in oil and food prices.

The emergence of sub-prime loan losses began the crisis and exposed other high-risk loans and over-inflated asset prices. With losses mounting and the collapse of the Lehman Brothers on September 15, 2008, a major panic spread across the international banking and loan market. As share and real estate prices immediately declined, we witnessed the collapse of the housing market. Many well-established investment and commercial banks in the United States and Europe suffered huge losses and faced bankruptcy, resulting in massive public financial assistance.

The bailouts began with the US government handing over billions to Fannie Mae and Freddy Mac, AIG, General Motors, Citigroup, JPMorgan Chase, Wells Fargo, Chrysler, Goldman Sachs, Morgan Stanley, and hundreds more! All the while, everyday citizens watched the stock market plummet to unimaginable lows, forcing many to hold off on retirement, and with the sharp increase in oil and food prices, many had to come out of retirement and take on new jobs.

At its peak, the Dow Jones Industrial Average exceeded 14,000 points in October 2007, and by March 2009, it had dropped to a sickly 6,600 points. It has since recovered most of the decline. But many fear that is only an illusion, and that one day it will drop faster and lower than before—and without recovery.

As many lost faith in the stock market, they began to frantically seek out safe havens for their money, which led to the major increase in the value of gold and silver. With gold soaring higher than $1,800 an ounce and silver prices rising above $40 an ounce, many investors believe there is still plenty of room for price increase—with silver more than gold, as it has been suppressed and, if corrected, should actually be more than $130 an ounce.

Many people began to save any pre-1965 quarters and dimes that were in their pockets because before 1965, these coins were minted with 90 percent silver content. The only coins minted by the United States that have actual value today are the one-dollar silver American eagles.

Think about this. Due to the devaluing of our dollar and increasing inflation, ten years ago, you could exchange a one-dollar bill for four pre-1965 quarters. Today, it will cost you a twenty-dollar bill for those four silver quarters. If you're lucky enough to come across one of these pre-1965 coins in your change, you just found five dollars' worth of silver, and you can exchange it anywhere coins are bought and sold.

Some economic analysts, weighing in at the beginning, declared that our nation's economy would hit rock bottom and that the government's attempt to fix the problem was only going to slow the process so that it would not be a sudden and devastating drop that would plunge us into chaotic darkness. As time has gone by, this certainly seems to have been the most accurate forecast we heard.

The most damaging decision for the US dollar came with quantitative easing,[1] an unconventional monetary policy used by central banks to stimulate the national economy when monetary policies begin to fail. A central bank implements quantitative easing by purchasing financial assets from banks and other private-sector businesses with new money that has been created out of thin air. One of the biggest risks in doing this is the possibility of high inflation—or, worse yet, hyperinflation.

In November 2008, the Federal Reserve, which is a privately owned entity and not actually a federal one, began buying $600 billion worth of mortgage-backed securities.[2] By March 2009, it held $1.75 trillion worth of bank debt and treasury notes, and it reached a peak in June 2010 with $2.1 trillion. As it soon became evident the economy was not recovering, in November 2010, the Fed announced a second round of quantitative easing, or QE2.[3] In doing so, they bought $600 billion worth of treasury securities by the end of the second quarter of 2011.

Economic analysts have stated that since QE2, the

stock market has increased significantly and, in turn, has boosted consumer confidence and increased spending. And this is where it is most evident that the rising stock market is only an illusion, because a false sense of security has boosted confidence with the injection of money that was created out of thin air. As we create more and more dollars, it doesn't take a rocket scientist to figure out that they become more and more useless.

As a result of our financial crisis and quantitative easing, China, along with other world powers, became very nervous with the status of the US dollar. Many began to discuss the prospects of a new world reserve currency, and many began calling for a replacement of the United States dollar. Many nations started trading with their own currencies, whereas before they were using the dollar. If—and more likely when—this happens, it will have devastating effects on the American economy.

Since the United States has the world reserve currency, all other countries are required to convert their currency to the US dollar to purchase oil. Having the world reserve currency, we have the benefit of a discounted price from OPEC when purchasing oil. But if we lose that status, our oil prices would significantly increase—and that would have unbearable consequences on the state of our already fragile economy. Yet as time goes on, we hear more and more presidents and world powers calling for the end of the reign of the dollar.

At home, as a result of the economic downturn, many people became short of funds, as they began paying more for gasoline and food while big banks and Wall Street firms reaped the benefits of government bailouts. The once middle class soon found itself counted among the poor, as companies and employers began to lay off large numbers and initiated hiring freezes and wage freezes. The cost of living continued to climb, while the income of many declined, thus making reality of the statement *The rich get richer, and the poor get poorer.*

With so many people being caught by the surprise of the sudden financial crisis, the losses were astronomical. With the loss of hard assets as well as liquid assets, many were depending on any savings they had to counter the effects of price inflation. Many who were obviously in denial, somewhat due to the media deceivingly saying the worst was over, continued to live beyond their means and dig themselves deeper into debt with the use of credit cards and other unsecured debt. In doing so, millions of Americans were left with no alternative but to file bankruptcy.

The consequences of the financial crisis to date have resulted in the foreclosure of nearly 5 million American homes.[4] Many having had their savings wiped out and, combined with a loss of income, were left homeless with nowhere to go. This forced many families to sell their personal belongings and pack what they could fit into their vehicles. The most important item that was packed was their new home: their family camping tent.

With what has been called "tent cities" popping up all over the nation, many people who once took for granted modern luxuries now found themselves fortunate just to eat a hot meal. As many family members turned to relatives for shelter, what were once single-family homes have now become multi-family homes. And with many simply not having any spare room, due to the fact that their adult children with college degrees moved back in, there were no options left than to turn to the tent cities. Being turned away by already overcrowded homeless shelters, they were informed of campground and park areas that had growing communities of families who were living in tents. Day-to-day life in these communities consists of gathering firewood, cooking food donated by local churches on outdoor grills, taking turns using the toilet and shower room, and listening to the news and ballgame updates on radios powered by portable generators.

Due to the growth of population in these tent cities, many county and city officials began a campaign to evict these citizens from the public camp and park areas. In 2007, St. Petersburg, Florida, gained recognition as one of the meanest cities in the nation when officials forcefully removed occupants from its tent city.[5] The police came to the site, informed everyone that they had to vacate the premises, and, armed with box cutters, began cutting and slashing all the tents that were not immediately taken down.

After the loss of many jobs and unemployment sky-rocketing to nearly 25 million Americans, the federal government extended the amount of time one could collect unemployment insurance. But even when that ran out, the only jobs to be found were mostly minimum wage, which produces an income that is nearly impossible to support a family. Due to this, among other various reasons, there are currently more than 22.4 million households on food stamps.[6] Considering there are approximately 82 million families in the US, this means that 15 percent of the population in America receives food assistance from the government. And the number of food-stamp recipients only continues to grow. If we look back at 2008, the number of people on food stamps was 29 million. The number in 2004 was only 22 million.

No good news can be found when researching our increasing amount of national debt, which hit $16 trillion dollars by late 2012. The amount recently surpassed our national GDP by more than $500 billion.[7]

Believe it or not, one thing that has helped keep our economy afloat is the major increase in the sale of fire-arms.[8] With Americans being so unsure of the outcome of the crisis and the fact that we have a liberal president (there were deep concerns that President Obama may pass harsh gun laws if he was elected for a second term), the economic impact of firearm sales hit $31 billion in 2011. Up from $19 billion in 2008, according to the National Shooting Sports Foundation.

Much like the saying *Misery loves company*, the pain we have felt at home has been the same experience for most everyone else across the world. In early 2010, the European Union, which is a confederation made up of twenty-seven member states in Europe, began to experience their sovereign debt crisis. Soon they created a rescue package worth $750 billion to ensure stability across Europe.[9] But this proved to have little effect. The Eurozone leaders agreed on more measures designed to prevent the collapse of member economies, and this included an agreement whereby banks would accept a 53 percent write-off of Greek debt owed to private creditors.[10] While sovereign debt has risen in several Eurozone countries, it has become a large problem for the area as a whole. In April 2010, the Greek government requested an additional loan of 45 billion euros from the EU and the International Monetary Fund to cover its financial needs for the remainder of the year.[11]

Less than a week later, Standard & Poor's slashed Greece's sovereign debt rating to BB+ or "junk status" amid fears of default. In the event of a default, investors were liable to lose as much as 50 percent of their money.

This news caused stock markets worldwide, as well as the European currency, to dramatically decline.

In May 2010, the Greek government announced a series of austerity measures to secure a three-year, 110-billion-euro loan. This caused great anger amongst the Greek public, leading to massive protests, riots, and social unrest throughout Greece. Riot police combated large numbers of protesters as they were attacked with rocks and Molotov cocktails. Headlines on the Internet read "Greece burns!" and businesses were set afire from the chaotic unrest.

Other countries began to experience similar problems. Among these countries was Ireland. Irish banks lost an estimated 100 billion euros due to defaulted loans to property developers and homeowners during the property bubble, which burst in 2007. And with the collapse of the economy in 2008, unemployment rose from around 4 percent to 14 percent in 2010. The federal budget went from a surplus in 2007 to a deficit of 32 percent GDP in 2010, even despite the austerity measures.

While Ireland could have guaranteed bank deposits and allowed private bondholders who had invested in the banks to suffer their losses, they instead borrowed money from the European Central Bank to pay these bondholders—which shifted the losses and debt to the taxpayers. This brought much attention to the creditworthiness of Ireland. As a result, the government started negotiations with the EU, the IMF, and three countries, including the United Kingdom, Denmark, and Sweden, which resulted in a $67.5 billion bailout agreement in late 2010.

PROTESTS IN THE MIDDLE EAST

As the recession remains with us, we have seen many changes in the world around us, with possibly the biggest changes being in the Middle East with the protests and rebellion known as the "Arab spring" or the "Arab uprising." It all started with street protests caused by high unemployment, food inflation, lack of freedoms, and poor living conditions, and it began in early December 2010, in Tunisia.

On December 17, 2010, Mohamed Bouazizi set himself on fire and burned to death in a show of extreme protest to these conditions.[12] The public's anger and violence following this act dramatically increased. The intensified protests led the president, Zine El Abidine Ben Ali, to step down on January 14, 2011, after twenty-three years in power.[13]

Seeing the success of the Tunisian uprising, protests began to spread like wildfire across the Arab nations. The next country to see major protest was Algeria, which led to the lifting of a nineteen-year-long state of emergency.[14] On January 14, 2011, protests began in Jordan, which led King Abdullah II to dismiss Prime Minister Samir Rifai and his cabinet.[15] On January 17, protests in Sudan led President Omar al-Bashir to announce he would not seek another term.

The next major protest started in Egypt on January 25, 2011. Less than three weeks later, the outcome was the overthrow of President Hosni Mubarak, who had been in power for more than thirty years.[16] Other significant outcomes of the Egyptian protests are as follows:

- Resignation of prime ministers

- Assumption of power by armed forces

- Suspension of the Constitution

- Dissolution of Parliament

- Takeover by Muslim Brotherhood

On February 19, 2011, protests in Kuwait led to the eventual resignation of Prime Minister Nasser Mohammed Al-Ahmed Al-Sabah.[17] Another protest began on January 27, 2011, in Yemen, which led to the overthrow of President Ali Abdullah Saleh in early February 2011.[18] Other results of the protest included:

- Resignation of prime minister

- Al Qaeda-linked militants took control of southern cities in Yemen

- Presidential election held to replace Saleh

In late August 2011, the government of Libya was overthrown. After refusing to step down, Muammar Gaddafi engaged military soldiers against rebel forces. He was killed by National Transitional Council forces on October 20, 2011.[19] The UN-mandated military intervention ended, and the NTC became the sole governing authority of Libya.

On March 15, 2011, protests began in Syria and, as of today, are still ongoing.[20] On April 17–18, 2011, thousands of protesters gathered in the central square of Homs, calling for the resignation of President Bashar al-Assad. When he refused to step down, protests continued and harsh security clampdowns and military operations began. By early December, the Baba Amr district of Homs fell under the armed Syrian opposition control. The armed Syrian opposition began to broaden its territory of control, fighting the Syrian army, which welcomed the help of 15,000 Iranian troops. While there is no official death toll as of yet, it is estimated that more than 11,000 civilians have been killed in the conflict. At the beginning of April 2012 a UN ceasefire agreement was presented, but troublesome conflicts continue to arise.

With presidents and governments across the Middle East being overthrown, there has been no evidence that daily life has become any easier for the people. Yet many inspired nations continue to challenge the authority of those ruling over them. Time will ultimately tell if this has been a positive victory or a pointless effort.

In the meantime, on September 17, 2011, America witnessed the birth of the Occupy Wall Street movement in the New York City financial district.[21] The protest was initiated by the Canadian activist group Adbusters and has led to Occupy movements across the nation. The issues of concern are social and economic inequality, corruption, greed, and the undue influence of corporations on government. Their slogan, "We are the 99%," refers to the growing income inequality between the wealthiest 1 percent in the nation and the rest of the population.

Those involved with the movement have stated that their goals are to have an increase in jobs, higher pay, bank reform, a reduction in the influence of corporations on politics, and forgiveness of student loan debt. While they have gained in numbers and continued to take over parks and camp out in business areas, there has been no sign that the movement will become hostile. However, the group has inspired others to consider the possibilities of more intense protesting. According to an April 6,

2012, *Washington Examiner* article, Van Jones, former White House czar, proclaimed that America in 2012 will witness its own "Arab spring."[22] He stated that the revolt will be launched in the spring with a war on corporate power, Wall Street greed, and political corruption. With more than 900 planned protest training sessions scheduled, the group will train and then begin their offensive against government and financial centers. While many had hoped for the American version of the "Arab spring," it has not been realized. This is the kind of scenario for which many conspiracy theorists suggest the US government has been preparing for martial law. And it could explain the increase in military exercises being conducted in large cities around the nation. Let's hope this doesn't happen, for though they have had a change in their leadership, there is still much uncertainty in the Middle East.

As if there aren't enough problems to keep us awake at night, let's consider the most talked-about war that has never happened, which is the potential beginning of World War III: the Israel-Iran war. Do you recall the Bush administration considering an attack on Iran? Well, for many years now, we have increasingly heard that something has to be done immediately, and as of yet we have seen no military action. But will it soon be a reality? And if so, what could be the potential outcome?

A History of Iran's Nuclear Ambitions

The foundation was laid for Iran's nuclear program on March 5, 1957, with a proposed agreement for cooperation in research of atomic energy being announced under President Dwight Eisenhower's Atoms for Peace program. By 1967, the Tehran nuclear research center was established and run by the Atomic Energy Organization of Iran. Their research center was equipped with a US-supplied, 5-megawatt nuclear research reactor, which was fueled by highly enriched uranium. Iran signed the Nuclear Non-Proliferation Treaty in 1968 and ratified it in 1970, making Iran's nuclear program subject to IAEA verification.

In the 1970s, the shah approved plans to construct, with the help of the US, up to twenty-three nuclear power stations by the year 2000. In 1976, President Gerald Ford signed a directive offering Tehran a chance to buy and operate a US-built reprocessing facility for extracting plutonium from nuclear reactor fuel. The shah also signed a nuclear agreement with South Africa, under which Iranian oil money financed the development of South African fuel enrichment technology.

In October 1977, demonstrations against the shah were taking place, and thus a revolution was underway. Quickly developing into a campaign of civil resistance that was both partly secular and partly religious, it only intensified in 1978. After a year of resistance, which paralyzed the country, the shah sought exile and left Iran in January 1979. As a result of this, two weeks later, Ayatollah Khomeini returned to Tehran, where he was warmly greeted by millions of Iranians. This event is known as the Islamic revolution, and its outcome was the forming of the Islamic Republic.

After the 1979 revolution, most of the international nuclear cooperation with Iran was cut off. Kraftwerk Union stopped working on Iran's nuclear project in January 1979, with one reactor 50 percent complete and the other 85 percent complete. They fully withdrew from the project in July, stating they had not received payment from Iran, but other sources said it was due to pressure from the United States.

In the early 1980s, the Iranian government concluded that the country's nuclear development should continue. And so it did, as they informed the IAEA. In 1984, German intelligence reported that Iran may have a nuclear bomb within two years with uranium supplied from Pakistan. Later that year, US Senator Alan Cranston asserted that Iran was at least seven years away from being able to build its own nuclear bomb.

In the early 1990s, Russia formed a joint research organization with Iran, called Persepolis, which provided Iran with Russian nuclear experts and technical information. Five Russian institutions, including the Russian Federal Space Agency, helped Iran improve its missile technology. President Boris Yeltsin had a two-track policy offering commercial nuclear technology to Iran and discussing the issues with Washington.

In 1995, Iran signed a contract with Russia to resume work on the partially complete Bushehr nuclear power plant, installing a pressurized water reactor. On August 14, 2002, an Iranian dissident group publicly revealed the existence of two nuclear sites that were currently under construction: a uranium enrichment facility in Natanz, part of which is underground, and a heavy-water facility in Arak. The IAEA immediately sought access to these facilities and further information from Iran regarding its nuclear program.

On August 31, 2006, President George W. Bush insisted there must be consequences for Iran's defiance of demands that it stop enriching uranium. He asserted, "The world now faces a grave threat from the radical regime in Iran."

The Iranian regime funds, arms, and advises Hezbollah, a Shia Muslim terrorist group.

Since 2006, the UN Security Council has passed seven resolutions on Iran, and we have since seen harsh economic sanctions on Iran for its lack of cooperation regarding its nuclear program. The latest report from the IAEA in November 2012 stated that Iran did not settle outstanding issues, nor did it permit the inspection of certain nuclear sites. And in televised speeches and interviews, Iran continues to insist that nothing will stop them from developing this further.[23]

A HISTORY OF IRAN'S HATRED FOR THE JEWS

Since the Islamic revolution in 1979, Iran has made perfectly clear that it has much hatred toward Israel and the Jewish people. At the very base of Iranian hatred toward the Jews and Israel is the fact that Iranians are predominantly Shia Muslim, which are more radical than the Sunni Muslims. And we know that in Islam, dating back to Muhammad himself, the Jews have always been considered an enemy to Islam. From a young age, the Shia Muslims are taught in their mosques that Jews are pigs and unworthy parasites.

With the declaration of Israel becoming a sovereign nation in 1948 and the Jewish people returning to their homeland, this exceedingly fueled Iran's hatred for not only the Jewish state, but also the West and America. To this day, Iran does not consider Israel a legitimate sovereign nation, and they most commonly refer to Israel as Palestine. In considering this, Iran believes the Jews have taken control of property that is not theirs and have forced the Palestinians from their own land. They believe the Jews are merely occupying Palestinian territory.

Since becoming president of Iran in 2005, President Mahmoud Ahmadinejad has repeatedly stated that the nation of Israel should be wiped off the map. As a result of his hate, he has made many public statements that would be very unbecoming of a president whose nation is seeking nuclear weapons. Below is a list of Ahmadinejad's quotes:

> If the killing of Jews in the Holocaust is true and the Zionist are being supported because of this excuse, why should the Palestinian nation pay the price?
>
> —PUBLISHED ON IRANIAN STATE TELEVISION'S WEBSITE ON DECEMBER 13, 2005

> Israel must be wiped off the map. The establishment of the Zionist regime was a move by the world oppressor against the Islamic world.
>
> —RECORDED IN AN ADDRESS TO 4,000 STUDENTS AT A PROGRAM TITLED "THE WORLD WITHOUT ZIONISM" ON OCTOBER 26, 2005

> Israel is destined for destruction and will soon disappear.
>
> —NOVEMBER 13, 2006

> Israel is a regime based on evil that cannot continue and one day will vanish.
>
> —RECORDED AT A STUDENT RALLY IN JAKARTA, INDONESIA, ON MAY 11, 2006

> With God's help, the countdown button has been pushed by the hands of the children of Lebanon

and Palestine....By God's will, we will witness
the destruction of this regime in the near future.
—Reported by the Fars News Agency on June
3, 2007

The list of quotes go on and on, but from these few we
can certainly determine that Iran has an agenda to attack
the nation of Israel. Iran has continued to proclaim that
its nuclear endeavors are peaceful, and yet it is a proven
fact that the nation supports terrorist groups. Even the
president himself publicly calls for the destruction of
Israel. President Ahmadinejad is a devout Muslim, who
believes he has a part to play in fulfilling Islamic prophecy
and that to enter the end of the age and bring about their
prophesied Mahdi, there must first be a great war with
the Zionists and the West. Likewise, we as Christians
know that the Bible speaks of such wars in the last days,
regarding the nation of Israel, in which God Himself will
intervene on Israel's behalf.

So, we know the United States ended World War II with
the drop of a bomb. Will we start World War III with the
drop of a bomb? As the days go by, Israel increasingly
implies it is very likely to take action with a military strike
on Iran's nuclear facilities. They have tirelessly attempted
to convince America to strike, but President Obama has
continually insisted that we let economic sanctions take
more time, in the hopes that the Iranians will abandon
their nuclear ambitions, though they have vowed that they
will never do so.

Recently, with the talk of a military strike on Iran's
nuclear facilities, Iran has warned that the consequences
of such an attack would be disastrous for Israel and the
West. They have said they would respond by launching

tens of thousands of missiles into Israel[24] and attacking American bases worldwide, as well as hitting key targets in America. Also, Iran has begun to threaten the closure of the Strait of Hormuz, which would cut off crucial oil supply, therefore creating a devastating impact on the US economy.

Both Israel and the US have recently conducted military training exercises to prepare for an attack on Iran. Likewise, Iran has been conducting military drills in anticipation of such an attack. Russia has stated that it will support Iran and stand firmly beside them in the event of an attack on Iran's nuclear sites. Russia has gone so far to say that it would consider such an attack on Iran as an attack on itself and that it would respond with military action.

In my online search of prophecies concerning America given by modern-day prophets, I came across one that struck me as being genuine from a man who was, no doubt, in touch with God. After hearing his testimony and prophecy, I began to make very interesting connections between what he prophesied in the 1980s and things that are developing on the world stage today.

The prophet's name was Dumitru Duduman,[25] and he was born in 1932 in Romania. He grew up a Christian, raised by a Christian family, and joined the marines after graduating from military school, with the rank of lieutenant. During his service, over the course of several years, he helped missionaries smuggle many Bibles into Romania and more than 300,000 Bibles into Russia. He said the Lord had sent an angel to him, and he commanded the angel to see that the missionaries were not caught.

After much success in his efforts, Duduman came under suspicion and constant surveillance. He was eventually arrested on suspicion and spent five months in jail, even though the authorities had no evidence against him. During this time, he was tortured in many ways as they tried to get him to confess to the crime. The man in charge of his tortures finally decided to just kill him but dropped dead of natural causes just before doing so. Through this act of God, Dumitru was set free.

After recovering from his injuries, Dumitru faithfully continued to do the work of God. Years later, he and his family were expelled from Romania by Communist officials. They traveled to Italy, where they stayed a short time, and eventually, in 1984, ended up in America. He was sad to find that America wasn't the nation of godliness he had always envisioned, and, not being able to speak English, things were exceptionally hard for him.

But once again, the angel of the Lord came to him while he was feeling low. The angel told him that God had brought him to America to prophesy to the people. The angel took him up on a device and showed him California, Las Vegas, Florida, and New York. He told Dumitru that all these places were a "Sodom and Gomorrah" and that they were going to burn. The angel went on to say that many people in America have left God and that in the church there is divorce, abortion, adultery, sodomy, and every other sin and that God would not live in sin.

The angel told Dumitru to tell the American people that Russian spies have learned the location of America's largest nuclear plants and that while there is peace in the nation, certain groups from the middle of the country will revolt against the government. While the government is occupied with this uprising, America will be caught off guard with bombings on these nuclear sites by invading planes that come in from Mexico, Cuba, Nicaragua, and other directions. In one day, America would burn.

Now, for a man of God to prophesy such an event in the 1980s, we should consider it as a possibility. But to see a scenario today that clearly matches his prophecy, we should consider it a very real probability. The Occupy movements in America, which have sought to become more aggressive, could be the revolt he described. It is also very interesting that we are considering bombing Iran's nuclear sites. Could his prophecy of our nuclear sites being bombed be an act of retaliation for an American or Israeli strike on Iran? He also mentioned Russian spies, and we know Russia has said they will support Iran in the event of a war with the West.

Without a doubt, things are looking rather grim for us, as well as the rest of the world. As circumstances continue to worsen—due to financial problems, if nothing else—it is a good opportunity to humble ourselves and grow closer to the Lord.

Chapter 7

APOCALYPSE AND ARMAGEDDON

THERE IS A common misconception today regarding the word *apocalypse*. Whenever the word comes up, which it increasingly does, it is usually describing a single event that will take place. We commonly hear of scenarios, such as a plague that will erase mankind or a meteor strike that will destroy all life or even the "Zombie apocalypse." While we know there will be plagues in the future (as there have been in the past) and meteors hitting the earth (as there have been in the past), we can say with certainty there will be no zombies.

The Greek word for *apocalypse* is *apokalypsis*, and the meaning of the word is "lifting of the veil" or "revelation." It refers to futuristic events seen by prophets in the Bible, the most commonly known of which is the Book of Revelation, also called the Apocalypse of John and the Revelation of Jesus Christ, written by John the Apostle around the year AD 95, according to early tradition, while in exile on the island of Patmos.

The structure of Revelation consists of four successive groups of seven: the seven churches, the seven seals, the seven trumpets, and the seven bowl judgments. Mentioned twenty-four distinct times, the number seven seems to be of special significance in this book. The number seven is also considered to be the number of perfection in Christianity.

In addition, the number seven, when cut in half to three and a half, is also of special significance. Two witnesses are given power to prophesy 1,260 days, or three and a half years, according to the Hebrew year of 360 days. The two witnesses are then killed, and their bodies lay in the street for three and a half days. The woman clothed with the sun is protected in the wilderness for 1,260 days, or three and a half years, and the Gentiles tread the Holy City underfoot for forty-two months, or three and a half years. The beast is given authority to continue for forty two months, or three and a half years.

Revelation is possibly the most studied book of the Bible; many people have spent much of their lives attempting to make modern-day connections to the prophecies it reveals. For example, when John speaks of the whore of Babylon, many people believe he is speaking literally of the city of Babylon, which is located in Iraq. In this theory, they suggest that one day the city of Babylon will be rebuilt, repopulated, and a major world-renowned location. In the 1980s, this theory gained credibility when Saddam Hussein began spending millions of dollars to reconstruct the historical city,[1] but since before his death, there has been no further progress of significance.

There are also many people who believe the "whore of

Babylon" refers to the Roman Empire because of its persecution of Christians and based on Revelation 17:9, which states that the woman sits on seven mountains, which they identify as the seven hills of ancient Rome. Furthermore, this theory is based on the revelation that she is clothed in purple and scarlet, which are the colors the Catholic clergy wear.

Another theory is that the whore of Babylon is actually the United States of America. The Greek word for whore, or prostitute, is *porne*, and the connection has been made with the porn industry that was created in America and still operates today. The case is also made from Revelation 17:15, which says, "Then he said to me, 'The waters which you saw, where the harlot sits, are peoples, multitudes, nations, and tongues'" (NKJV). This is suggested to be in reference to the diverse national background of citizens in the United States and the diverse number of languages that we speak. There are also various verses in Revelation that speak of fornication, which has led many to believe that the verses are in reference to the worldwide distribution of pornography.

Many connections linking the whore of Babylon with America are also found in earlier books of the Bible. I have included five interpretations of verses that have led many to believe this theory:

- Babylon is deep in the occult, in sorceries, which are also believed to be a reference to drug use (Isa. 47:12).

- Babylon is a coastal nation that sits upon many waters (perhaps referring to our rivers?) and is abundant with treasures (Jer. 51:13).

81

- Babylon would be a home to many Jews who leave (Jer. 50:4–6).

- Babylon would be youngest and greatest of end-time nations (Jer. 50:12).

- Babylon would be the hammer of the whole earth (Jer. 50:23).

And if we take seriously the words of Dumitru Duduman, who prophesied that Russian spies would provide the locations of America's nuclear sites for a military strike, we can directly connect this verse:

> For behold, I will raise and cause to come up against Babylon an assembly of great nations from the north country, and they shall array themselves against her; from there she shall be captured. Their arrows shall be like those of an expert warrior; none shall return in vain.
>
> —JEREMIAH 50:9, NKJV

The word "arrows" in this verse may allude to precision-guided missiles.

Another interesting connection that has been made between Babylon and the United States is the similarity between America's Statue of Liberty and the Babylonian statue of Ishtar, both of which hold a torch in their right hands and a book in their left hands.

The most convincing evidence for America being Babylon is a verse that jumped out at me while studying the Book of Revelation. Let me ask you: What color comes to mind when I say the words *fine linen*? If your answer is white, you are correct. Fine linen is linen in its purest form that has not been dyed or mixed with any other color. In the Book of Revelation, John describes the saints as wearing fine linen that is pure and white.

Now, what is the only color that can be mistaken for purple? If your answer is blue, or a deep blue, you are correct.

What color is scarlet? If your answer is red, or blood red, you are correct.

Finally, what nation today owns the most gold and has the largest gold reserve in the world? If your answer is America, you are correct.

Now, let us look at the verse that clearly describes the American flag and the fact that we have the most gold:

> And saying, Alas, alas, that great city, that was
> clothed in fine linen, and purple, and scarlet, and
> decked with gold, and precious stones, and pearls!
>
> —REVELATION 18:16

The way John says "fine linen, and purple, and scarlet" clearly tells me he is describing fine linen as a color—he did not say fine linen that was purple and scarlet, but rather describes it as a color with the key word here being *and.*

While there are many opinions that comprise sound theories, we know that one day we will eventually be able to clearly discern such prophecies. Among the judgments that will come upon the whole earth, one of great consequence will be the star Wormwood, which is prophesied as bringing much death to mankind:

> And the third angel sounded, and there fell a great
> star from heaven, burning as it were a lamp, and
> it fell upon the third part of the rivers, and upon
> the fountains of waters; and the name of the star
> is called Wormwood: and the third part of the
> waters became wormwood; and many men died
> of the waters, because they were made bitter.
>
> —REVELATION 8:10–11

While some believe this description to be symbolic of a nuclear disaster that would pollute our waters, some believe it could also be an event where satellites or space stations fall to the earth and somehow contaminate the waters. But if we consider the words of the verse, where it states that a "Great star" falls from heaven, we should believe it to be a massive meteor. But how could a single star fall on a third of the waters? And how could it contaminate them?

To answer that question, let me tell you this story. My wife, Miryah, recently had a troubling dream that seemed to be both a warning and a prophecy. In her dream, the two of us and our children were traveling south when we started to experience severe earthquakes. As they intensified, making it hard to drive, we turned back and headed home. In doing so, we had to stop for gas. While we were stopped, she noticed an object in the sky that she identified as being the moon, as it was nighttime. She also saw a strange red sphere around the moon, and suddenly it appeared to explode and then the moon was gone.

When this happened, she demanded that I get back in our SUV and leave. As we were leaving, she said that we experienced a violent thrust forward, like when you are pushed from behind unexpectedly. She witnessed all the trees of the forest, which were a distance from the highway, bend down from this force. Then the sky was bright, as if the sun had suddenly and unexpectedly risen, and there was a sudden heavy snowfall that began to accumulate all over the ground around us.

After waking up, Miryah was very troubled by the dream and we began our attempt to understand it. After studying the dream, we saw that it obviously involved a cosmic event that had serious effects on the earth. Together, we came to the conclusion that what appeared to be the moon was possibly a star coming near to the earth. Being so near, if it were a "great star," it would appear to be the size of the moon.

We presume if this were to actually happen, it is possible that world powers would agree to strike it with a nuclear weapon. If a nuclear blast were to take place in the atmosphere, this could explain the sudden light she saw, as though the sun had risen unexpectedly. And the snowfall in her dream could represent a nuclear winter. As a possible result of the star being hit with a nuclear weapon, it would break up into many smaller pieces, both covering and contaminating many waters.

Now, this dream could represent any number of other things, but we thought this interpretation was interesting. I have also considered her dream to be like the description of the day of the Lord as it is described in Zechariah 14:7: "It shall be one day which is known to the LORD—neither day nor night. But at evening time it shall happen that it will be light" (NKJV).

Another judgment that will have massive effects on mankind will come in the form of a great famine:

> And when he had opened the third seal, I heard the third beast say, Come and see. And I beheld, and lo a black horse; and he that sat on him had a pair of balances in his hand. And I heard a voice in the midst of the four beasts say, A measure of wheat for a penny, and three measures of barley for a penny; and see thou hurt not the oil and the wine.
>
> —REVELATION 6:5–6

Many people are concerned about the theory that says we will soon no longer be able to feed everyone on the earth, especially since the global population has more than doubled in just the last forty years. We also know that according to prophecy many people shall starve to death. It would be quite foolish to think that America and other superpowers would be excluded from such a judgment. And this could happen at a moment's notice, taking the masses by surprise.

Let's imagine that a catastrophic event takes place

tomorrow morning that shuts down all manner of food production and delivery. The stores are overrun by belligerent consumers across the nation that decimate all remaining food supplies in less than twenty-four hours, leaving the common citizen to make do with whatever remains from their last trip to the grocery store.

How long would it be before millions of hungry stomachs turned on each other, killing one another for food that is no longer available to the masses? A growing number of American citizens are preparing for an event like this by stocking up on food items that will keep their family fed while others watch their children starve to death for their lack of preparation.

There are instances in the Bible where a famine on the land was prophesied so that necessary measures could be taken to prevent starvation. So, with many becoming prepared and carefully considering the worst-case scenario, could this allude to something horrible being on the horizon? Or is it just something in the air?

We certainly know that if something horrible does happen, those who have prepared for an uncertain future will thank God they did. And those who go hungry will certainly have themselves to blame when they resort to begging and stealing from those who have food. We see a clear description of this in the Apocrypha:

> Sown places shall suddenly appear unsown, and full storehouses shall suddenly be found to be empty.
>
> —2 Esdras 6:22

> A man shall have no pity upon his neighbors, but shall make an assault upon their houses with

> the sword, and plunder their goods, because of
> hunger for bread and because of great tribulation.
>
> —2 ESDRAS 15:19

> And those who are in the mountains and high-
> lands shall perish of hunger, and they shall eat
> their own flesh in hunger for bread and drink
> their own blood in thirst for water.
>
> —2 ESDRAS 15:58

The Apocrypha—which in Greek means "those which were hidden"—is a series of books that describe the end times. While not considered today to be part of the canon of Scripture, these books were included in all versions of the Christian Bible before 1828. And many point out that the most common Bible in the days of Jesus was the Greek translation, also called the Septuagint, which included these texts.

Among these judgments, we know that we will see many others, such as plagues and many wars that kill billions of people. But another common misconception is the meaning of the word *Armageddon*. In Hebrew, it is *Har Megiddo*, which literally means "Mount Megiddo." It is a location twenty-five miles southwest of the southern tip of the Sea of Galilee, in the Kishon river area. In 1998, the film *Armageddon* suggested that an asteroid was headed to earth and that if it was not stopped, the result would be "Armageddon." Spoken of by John in the Book of Revelation, it is the location where the final battle will take place and the Antichrist will be defeated by Jesus Christ:

> For they are the spirits of devils, working miracles,
> which go forth unto the kings of the earth and of

the whole world, to gather them to the battle of
that great day of God Almighty.

—REVELATION 16:14

And he gathered them together into a place in the
Hebrew tongue Armageddon.

—REVELATION 16:16

It will be the war to end all wars and the end of man's
government on earth and the beginning of Christ's righ-
teous government. Many wars, plagues, and famines lead
up to this final battle, so if someone suggests that an event
called Armageddon will happen soon without having seen
all these things take place first, they are greatly mistaken.

Chapter 8

IN MY DARKEST HOUR, GOD SAID, "LET THERE BE LIGHT"

HAVING BEEN RAISED with a Christian foundation, I am forever thankful to my family. I cherish memories of my grandparents, who were devoted Christians. My grandfather on my mother's side, Woodrow Talley, not only attended the Assembly of God, but would also hold church and prayer meetings at his home, which was within short walking distance of where I grew up. I even recall him helping start a Church of God in Wright City, Missouri, with a great minister named John Riley.

My memories of my grandmother, his wife, Chloie, are those of a saintly woman who bore him eight children and labored tirelessly to maintain their home and always had a genuine smile on her face. Having created a large family, many good, Christian, God-fearing people are my relatives. Though not all of us attend church, as we were taught we should do, I take this opportunity to insist that we start.

Having married my beautiful wife, Miryah, when I was eighteen, who reminds me so much of my grandfather's wife, we started our own family and bought a house. Sadly, I did not carry on the traditions of my heritage by attending church. As years went by, I continued to grow only further from the example that had been set for me, instead finding it common to drink alcohol, listen to heavy rock music with ungodly lyrics, find much amusement in horror films, and consider only the pleasures of this world.

The signs were there all along that God wasn't pleased with the way I was living. I would often have strong feelings come over me when going out for drinks with a friend. Sudden fear would at times strike me, yet I would still buckle under peer pressure. There were unexplainable noises in the house that we considered to be ghosts. The activity would usually consist of a thump on the wall or the sound of footsteps creaking the hardwood steps that led up to our bedroom. Our house, when we bought it, was nearly a hundred years old, so we assumed the ghost of a past resident was occasionally letting us know they were still there. Looking back now, I recall the noises to have been most common during the time I was drinking and sinning on a regular basis.

Several years passed with very little activity in the house. By this time, we had three children and I had stopped going out drinking, but we were still without God in my household. Though I occasionally studied the Bible and repented for my sins, I had certainly not overcome them.

Due to the nature of my wife's upbringing, she was not as familiar with Christianity as was I, so we didn't speak much of the topic, especially as I was all but convinced she would never come around, so to speak. I didn't push the subject on her, because I knew she had anger and confusion in her heart due to the untimely and tragic loss of a sibling. So we seemed to be coasting along in life, doing as well as anyone and without God in our life.

In the year 2010, though, I began to have recurring nightmares about tornadoes. These dreams would sometimes include as many as four or five tornadoes at a time, coming at me from all directions and leaving me totally hopeless by the end of the dream. These troubling dreams only added to the misery of the recession we were in, as I had to work twelve hours a day in extreme heat at a job that required a two-hour commute.

I found myself increasingly unhappy, and not just due to my work. Looking back now, I realize I had a strong spirit of depression over me. Having witnessed the end of the year, I considered it to be the worst year of my life, and I convinced myself to once again become optimistic about the future.

It was not the optimism I needed, though, which was spiritual; rather, it was the optimism of materialism. Against my better judgment, and with my wife not objecting, we decided to finance a late-model sports car. At the same time, we bought my wife a tattoo starter kit so that she could learn a new and profitable trade.

After a few weeks went by, it became obvious that to keep up with our bills, considering the addition of the sports car, she would have to take on a full-time job. By early March, she had been hired by a company that owns and operates a tree orchard. This created a very hectic schedule for us, as I was working from 7 p.m. to 7 a.m. and she was working from 7 a.m. to 3:30 p.m. Considering that the location of my job was an hour from home, I had to work exceedingly hard to finish a twelve-hour job in ten and a half hours, just to get home in time for her to leave so that the children would not be alone and so I could get them ready for school.

As another several weeks went by, it seemed to be working. We weren't seeing much of each other, but we had the bills paid and extra money in our pockets. She was making unbelievable progress in her tattoo training, and I was adding tattoos to myself as well. We soon agreed that we were going to save up money for one year and then open a tattoo shop. It seemed to be a great idea. We could quit our factory jobs and independently run our own business, and we would be able to spend all of our time together.

Soon, we began to experience extreme weather, and there were tornadoes popping up everywhere. There were even a few tornadoes less than a mile from our house. I had since forgotten my warning dreams about tornadoes and hadn't even made any connection between them.

As a result of the extreme weather, both our SUV and our new sports car were severely damaged by large hail—not only on one occasion, but numerous times during a span of about two months. As soon as we would get the damage repaired and leave the shop, we would have another hailstorm. We even had a hailstorm while the cars were in the shop and we were driving a rental car! After all damage repairs were finished, we had totaled up more than $10,000 in insurance claims.

We were exceedingly tired from our schedule, and we missed our quality time together, but we had a plan to better ourselves financially, so we thought it best to rough it out for a year. However, my spirit of depression soon returned to me. The long hours at work and rushing to get home to see the kids off quickly took its toll on me physically, and the loneliness of the empty house and empty bed when I would go to sleep took its toll emotionally.

My wife suffered from the same issues and the added labors of housework and taking care of the children all evening by herself. I began to again express my hatred for life and how I would rather be dead at times. I soon proclaimed that 2010 was, in fact, not the worst year of my life—now it was 2011, without a doubt. It had taken me no time at all to learn that a financially comfortable life was not worth living if you had to rush home every day only to find an empty house.

Soon I began to have troubling dreams again, except this time, with my wife at work and the children in school, I had no one to take comfort in when waking from them. Around this same time, my wife began experiencing an increase in stomach pains, and she began to experience dramatic and sudden weight loss. We were both very concerned that she had a serious condition. But being afraid of finding out some worst-case scenario from the doctor, she decided to first change her diet and see if that helped. About the same time, I developed the worst sinus infection I had ever had, and it stayed with me through three runs of antibiotics and more than three months.

My troubling dreams continued, and a common theme emerged: that Miryah and I were divorced. This bothered me, and I began seeking reassurance from her that we were OK and that a divorce was completely out of the question. As we talked, she assured me that it was only a bad dream, most likely brought on by stress. I began to question our schedule, as well as our intentions of opening a tattoo shop, for I began to feel that it was not the lifestyle that we should create for ourselves or our children.

One evening in particular, I recalled that my wife had

a pack of tarot cards in her dresser, which she'd had since an early teenager. Being curious as to what they might predict—and never having subscribed to such things before—I asked that she give me a reading concerning my future. As I somewhat expected, the answers were as disturbing as my dreams. They strongly implied that I would soon find myself divorced and without our possessions.

This prediction only intensified my worries. Still, she admitted a divorce was out of the question and that the cards weren't necessarily accurate.

Then one morning in mid-August, I awoke from a dream that was unshakable. I saw in the dream my wife in bed with another man, who looked to be older, maybe in his early forties. Now the worried state I was in became a state of horror. I couldn't shake the vision of this, nor get it out of my head.

I've had jealous tendencies in the past because I love my wife more than I could ever explain, and the thought of losing her kills me. I was sure of her devotion to me, and I also knew that even if she wasn't devoted, she certainly didn't have time to engage in an affair.

Still, I thought this dream may be a warning that someone was beginning to trespass into our marriage and become a wedge between the two of us for their own gain. So I asked her if there was someone she was talking to, that she please tell me, that she put it on the table and decide what she wanted to do. In the hopes that she would be honest, I assured her that I would not start screaming and breaking things if the answer was yes.

But her answer was no. She was not talking to anyone, but she *was* thinking of leaving me. She explained that I had too often proclaimed that I hated my life, and since she was a major part of it, she felt that I also hated her.

She also thought that somehow, since I had become so unhappy, it was her fault. I explained to her that the only things I was unhappy about were my job and the lack of time we had together. We assured each other of our love and agreed that even if we were to change our schedule and accept the loss of possessions, the most important thing was that we stay together.

But as the weeks went by, we began to argue and fight almost on a daily basis. I grew increasingly suspicious of her and started questioning her about who she was texting, having snooped through her phone and discovered there were messages that had been erased.

One morning during the first week of October, she informed me that she had, in fact, been talking to a co-worker who happened to be a man that matched the description in my dream. She assured me he was only a friend and that there wasn't even an inappropriate discussion between them. But from my point of view, he was certainly interested in her, and his goal was obviously the outcome of my dream.

As I stated previously, years before I had spent much time out drinking with friends. Having committed adultery myself, which I asked forgiveness for, I knew well how men operate. This sent me into a rage, as I realized the dream to be a true revelation. We agreed that, due to the fact that all we could do with our little time that we had together was fight, we would call it quits and leave each other.

But before we could even leave each other's sight, even to go into another room, we reconciled. I knew the only way that God could get my attention was by a scenario like this, because I love my wife dearly, as well as our children, and so this was a near-death experience for my very soul.

That is when I realized my house had been out of order for much too long and that it was time to bring God into our lives. A few nights later, we sat down together on our couch and, after a few moments of discussion, agreed that we needed to seek God and get our family into church. At the very moment we decided this, we heard loud screams coming from upstairs. We stood up as our two daughters came running down the stairs and into the living room. They both had tears streaming down their faces and were trembling in fear.

When we asked what was wrong, they screamed that there were loud scratching noises on the walls of their bedroom. My wife looked at me, and we both realized that the ghosts in our house were something darker. In fact, they were demons. We immediately went upstairs to their room to inspect it, but we found nothing. Just the same, Miryah retrieved our family Bible and began to pray in the girls' bedroom.

We soon came to many conclusions. First, that not only was there something wicked in our home, but that it had been dictating our life with its unseen influence. I was very frightened, more so than my wife, because even though I had heard many sermons on demons and hellfire, I had not obeyed the Word of God. I began to feel a dark presence at the foot of my bed at night when I would try to get to sleep. I would see visions of horrible faces when my eyes were closed. One in particular that stood out was a blue-skinned face that looked like it was half-man, half-fish.

And then one night, after coming home from work around 3 a.m., I had a frightening experience after taking a shower. I was in the process of drying off with a towel when I heard a deep, throaty growl coming from the other side of the bathroom door. I was at first in shock from the sound, as I knew everyone was asleep and that even if they weren't, there was certainly no one in the house who could create that kind of noise. And not having a dog—or any animal of any kind in the house, for that matter—it could only be one thing.

I wrapped the towel around myself and quickly opened the door. There was nothing there. I quickly went upstairs to see if anyone was awake, but they were all in bed, asleep.

The next major incident was on a Saturday night. It was the night before our first Sunday morning church service as a family. We set our alarm on the computer in our room (because our alarm clock was broken), said our prayers, and turned out the lights around 10 p.m.

Sometime around 2 a.m., I sat up in bed. Something had woken me, and I could feel a presence at the foot of the bed, as though something dark and hateful was staring at my wife and me as we slept. However, this time I was no longer frightened, but I was angry, for had it not only tried to separate my family, but now it had been terrorizing us to make up for its failed attempts. And so I spoke out loud to it and commanded that it show itself to me, that I might attempt to battle it. But nothing appeared to me. I said a prayer and managed to fall back asleep.

Only four hours later, the demon showed itself to my wife. She had woken up and was lying in bed when she realized it was just starting to get light outside. She decided not to go back to sleep since it was close enough time to get up, and she decided she would get up and take a shower. But as she lay there thinking this, suddenly a strong vision overwhelmed her. She saw herself walk over to the bedroom window that overlooks our front yard from the second story. She saw a beast that was larger than a man, but with cat-like features and a long tail. It was covered in hair, and it had large, black eyes; she described them as looking into a dark void. It had a squirrel in its mouth that it was eating, and it seemed to notice her. It stood up and looked directly at her face.

It then quickly moved across the yard and out of her sight. Instantly, she heard loud steps move up and onto the porch, and she said, "It's coming in the house—no, it's already in the house!"

This vision, having terrified her, made her want to stay in bed, because she was afraid the beast may be in the house, as it was a powerful and very real vision. She continued to lie in bed a little longer, and then her bravery returned to her.

It was a good thing she was strong, because when she got up to cancel the alarm clock, she discovered the time on our computer had moved back two hours at some point in the night. If she had stayed in bed, as her frightful experience nearly persuaded her to do, the alarm would not have gone off in time for us to make it to church.

After she made this discovery, it was getting fairly light outside. Feeling confident it was only a vision, and no longer thinking that a beast was literally in the house, she went downstairs to take a shower. But while in the shower, she experienced a sudden chill and was instantly covered with goose bumps. The room was suddenly filled with an overwhelming smell of infection, as though someone with rotting teeth were breathing in her face. She immediately began to pray, saying the name "Jesus Christ" out loud, and when she did, the smell and the cold sensation went away.

After she got out of the shower, she returned upstairs to wake me and the children. I was the hardest to wake, because I was on a nightshift schedule, and so I told her I just wanted to stay in bed. I clearly remember her words that instantly motivated me to get up: "Fine, then. You can stay here with the thing I saw this morning while the children and I go to church."

And so we went to church at the First Assembly of God, where my sister Mary so faithfully attended. My parents attended, as well, to help support us. The senior pastor prayed for us, laying hands on us and asking God to be with us in our time of great trouble, and this lifted a great weight from our backs and boosted our faith level higher than ever. Our eyes were opening to the influence that was in our life, and our ears were opening to the Holy Spirit.

When we had returned home, we were at ease and felt refreshed. But we soon made a discovery we had not seen—or perhaps hadn't been able to see before. In a picture that I had recently taken of my wife and had posted on Facebook, my mother informed me there were very strange things around Miryah in the photo. Upon examining it, we saw a mist around her and what appeared to be a dark figure standing behind her on the porch, about the size of a man.

This visual evidence motivated us to inspect some other photos we had recently taken that year. Upon doing so, we found a photo I had taken of our son not long after the beginning of the year that absolutely shocked us. In the photo, he is standing in our upstairs hallway, smiling for the picture, but in the window behind him, a demon is peering inside with a horrible expression on its face. We couldn't believe what we were seeing.

A second photo was taken seconds after this one, and it

reveals the same demon but with a different expression on its face. We accepted the fact that since we had opened our eyes and ears, we were given revelation as to what was going on in our home, that had turned our lives upside down.

Above: Demon captured in photo with head back and mouth open, just below curtain. There also appears to be arms, a chest, and a belly in the bottom window frame.

Perhaps one of the greatest memories of my life was created around this time. My wife, Miryah, had bowed to her knees in prayer and accepted the Lord Jesus Christ as her Savior. She was healed of her illness, and her appetite, which she had lost for several months, immediately returned to her. She was absolutely glowing, and many people recognized this and confessed to her how well she suddenly looked. We began to talk about God for hours on end, feeling the Holy Spirit on us as we so joyfully engaged in discussion.

With all the revelations we experienced concerning the demonic forces at work in our home, we asked that a family member who recently became a minister come to our home and bless it for us. They were happy to do so, so we scheduled it for a week or so later.

Not having the powerful faith level that my wife had so quickly risen to, I was still frightful and worried about the outcome of events. We had experienced some bizarre occurrences in our home that were obviously of demonic nature. We desperately needed to better understand our circumstances, but we didn't know who we could talk to regarding them.

Around this time, we were searching for sermons on YouTube, seeking a word from the Lord, when I came across the man of God who forever changed our lives: Perry Stone. A fourth-generation minister, he is the director of the fastest-growing ministry in the world, Voice of Evangelism, and he holds the rank of ordained bishop at the Church of God in Cleveland, Tennessee.

As we began to watch Stone's recorded sermons, which dated as far back as 2008, we immediately received the answers we had been longing for. At times during his prophetic teaching, the Holy Spirit would lead him to preach on topics that didn't always fit the subject he was on. These were moments that answered many questions that we were asking. At times, it was obvious that God was speaking directly to us through His faithful servant. My wife and I would look at each other and smile in amazement. It was like we were on an open phone line with the church and Perry Stone was directly answering our questions.

I have never heard a minister deliver so much information in each and every sermon that they preach as Perry Stone does. He not only gives a word from the Lord, but he deciphers prophetic future events, as well as lessons on history as they relate to the Bible. After viewing a few of his sermons, the voice of Perry Stone was soon heard in our home every day. Having watched all the available material we could find, we would replay the sermons we had previously viewed. We have come to enjoy many of his books and DVD sets that are very informative and inspiring for today's Christian audience. I pray that God continues to bless this man and that he is able to continue reaching more and more people who need a word from the Lord.

Three weeks to the day that my wife had the vision of the beast in our yard, we came home from church and ate lunch. After doing so, we decided to replace a broken windowpane on the front of our house. I was chipping away at the old caulking so that the new windowpane would fit in the frame, when my wife took a turn and relieved me. As I took my break, I was leaning against one of the columns on our wraparound porch, when suddenly something in the yard caught my eye.

It was a dead squirrel, and I immediately remembered the vision of the beast with the squirrel in its mouth that had terrified my wife. I stepped down off the porch and went into the yard to closer examine it. Upon giving it a nudge with my foot, it was only slightly stiff, which told me that it had not been dead long. I then turned it over to inspect it for any wounds that may have caused its death and saw what looked like large puncture marks that you would find on the victim of a vampire in a Hollywood production.

After this discovery, I walked back onto the porch and hesitated to tell my wife—I didn't want to upset her, as she had been through so much already. But upon turning to speak to me, she could tell I was visibly shaken and asked what was the matter. I asked her that if there was a frightening revelation I discovered, would she want to know what it was? She answered yes, of course she would want to know.

My words were simply this. I said, "Look in the yard," and pointed my finger in the direction of the squirrel. She immediately saw it and turned her head with her hand over her open mouth. I then asked her, in the eleven years that we have lived here, have we ever discovered a dead animal of any kind in our yard? She answered what I already knew: No, never. We embraced one another for a moment, and I told her I would get rid of it. But she said no, that she would dispose of it herself.

After our embrace, she was smiling as though not having been startled at all. She said "How pathetic!" and gave a short laugh. I asked her to please explain herself. She said it was a laughable threat from the demon. In an attempt to scare us by providing evidence it was real, all it could do was leave a dead squirrel! She put the squirrel in a trash bag and, with a smile on her face, carried it around back and disposed of it.

We came to the conclusion that a dog in the neighborhood had probably killed it and left it in our yard, as we had recently learned demons can possess animals to do such things. We had finally had our home blessed, after eleven years of living in it, with the help of family members who had taken time out of their busy schedule to travel more than fifty miles to do so. The husband walked from room to room, saying a prayer in each one, and put oil on every doorway and on all seventeen window frames in the house.

Then he revealed to us that when he was praying in our bedroom, where I had often sensed a dark presence, he felt a heavy thickness in the air and experienced the sensation of being choked while he was praying. He concluded the blessing on our front porch, and we all agreed that the atmosphere in the house was more inviting. As he and his wife were leaving, we tried to provide him with money to pay for his gas, considering the long distance he had traveled, but he refused. And so we thanked him, and he and his wife left the house.

Before this man had blessed our house that day, we talked with him about the Lord, and he helped counsel me and my wife regarding the troubles we had experienced. Earlier that day, my uncle had stopped by to see the pictures of the demon captured in the window. He also gave counsel to us. What was amazing was that both men in their counsel said similar things—even some identical things—regarding our situation. At the end of the day, my wife and I agreed that the Lord was certainly speaking to us through them.

Unfortunately, my faith was still not at the level that my wife's was. I began to doubt all the evil spirits were gone, and so I worried and felt I was by no means out of the woods. Then late one evening, just before bedtime, I went to the bathroom to brush my teeth. As I was preparing to do so, I looked in the mirror and dropped my toothbrush as a result of what I seen. I saw myself dead. My skin was a pale blue, and I had very dark circles around my eyes. I looked like a body that had drowned and been pulled from a lake.

In disbelief, I looked down at my arms and hands to see if I had only appeared that way in the mirror, but to my horror, I was pale blue all over. I rushed to my wife to see if I only appeared this way to myself or if she could see me as though I was dead as well. I felt a little relief when she announced that I appeared to look normal to her.

I soon found myself increasing my prayers on my hour commute to work. Whereas I used to listen to loud rock music, the stereo was now silent. I would talk to God and surround myself in total silence to receive a word. I also began to carry one of my Bibles with me at all times. My faith level was getting stronger every day, and I feared less the things that sought my destruction and the separation of my family.

Having worked at the same place as my brother, as we had been hired on the same day nine years before, I always looked forward to our conversations. Upon discussing my troubles with him, he recommended I speak to a man that often came into our factory who not only owned a cleaning service but was also a minister in a nearby city. My brother said the man seemed to know a lot about the subject of angels and demons, as he had discussed such topics with him before.

The man's name is Jethro Hopgood, and he changed my life. Aside from saying, "Hi. How are you today?" to him in passing as I worked, I had not really had a conversation with him before. But a few nights later, I decided to seek his counsel, so I left the house about twenty minutes earlier than usual, in the hopes that he would be there when I arrived early—and he was.

I was a little nervous about unloading such a story on a man who was virtually a stranger to me, but when I entered the building, he first approached me and started a conversation. I took this as a sure sign from the Lord that I should speak to him concerning my troubles.

I first explained to him that I had been having strange things happen in my house and that I found a disturbing image in a photo taken there. I handed him the photo and asked if he saw anything strange in it, and if so, what did he see? He said, "It's a demon." Then he put his hand on me and said, "Tell me about the jealousy." I was shocked!

I told him about the situation with my wife, and then he asked what was going on with my father or her father. Again, I was shocked. I told him my wife had been out of contact with her father for more than ten years and that upon finding him on Facebook earlier in the year, I strongly encouraged her to make contact with him and rebuild a relationship. Then, when we were at the beginning phase of our troubles, we discussed the option of moving to Wisconsin, where her father lived, to start over fresh. Jethro advised me not to do so, at least not anytime soon.

Here, God was again speaking through another man, giving me the guidance and the answers I needed. After this, Jethro and I had many conversations about the Lord. I am forever thankful for his counsel and his knowledge that so helped me.

He advised me to get baptized, even if I were to do it at home myself. And so I did, the very next day. With my wife praying and holding the Bible, I recited what Jethro had told me to say, and I gave my heart to the Lord as I baptized myself in our bathtub.

A week or so later, while I was working, Jethro called me over to him and said he needed to talk to me. He said he had received a word from God about me. The Lord told him that his counseling of me was finished and that I now belonged to God. This made me very happy, but Jethro had also been given a revelation about the demon that had been haunting my steps. He said the demon felt I owed it something, and it wasn't going to leave until it got it.

This disturbed me, and after Jethro left, I began to worry a little. I asked myself, *What does the demon think I owe? Does it expect my soul? Or my life?* I told myself to have faith and began to think on other matters to rid it of my mind. I thought perhaps I would have Miryah cut my hair for me when I got home—and that is when I learned that not only could God speak through people without them being aware of it, but also demons could do the same.

In less than one minute of my having thought of getting

a haircut after work, one of my work buddies sat down next to me at break and asked, "Is it true that your hair keeps growing when you die?"

It had to be the demon suggesting that I was going to die and that I shouldn't bother with thoughts of getting a haircut. I asked him, "Why do you ask such an odd question out of the blue?"

He said, "I don't know. It just popped in my head when I walked over here."

I had finally gotten rid of my sinus infection after three months of misery, but there was a flu virus going around, and one by one, everybody in the house was getting sick. It started with our son, who was the youngest, and worked its way up to us by age. Since I was oldest, I was sick last.

The day that I came down with the flu was the first workday after Thanksgiving break. We always had Thursday and Friday off as a paid holiday, but if we did not attend work the day before or after, we were not paid for the holiday.

The flu virus had such an effect on me, I could not stand up straight or walk without vomiting on myself. So I had no option but to call in sick and request a sick day, which would not only allow me to keep my holiday pay, but it would also save a mark against my attendance. It was only later that I found out, upon receiving a small paycheck, that my sick day was not approved. While the much-needed money was not there, I wasn't too concerned about my attendance, as I had a discussion with one of the managers a month before who told me I would be safe if I needed to call in after November 16.

More than a month later, the week after Christmas, I was called into the office upon arriving at work and was told I was fired due to my attendance. When I pointed out

I was still safe according to the rules of attendance, the manager just shrugged his shoulders and said the decision was already made. I didn't protest. I admitted my attendance should have been better. I shook his hand and then left. Though I had been transformed by becoming saved, the bosses had not had a chance to know the new me. And so the old me had destroyed my only source of income.

When I arrived home with a piece of paper in my hand and my head hung low, only a little over two hours of being gone (two of those hours being road time), my wife comforted me and told me that the Lord was still working in our lives. And as a result of the extra time on my hands, I have enjoyed much-needed quality time with my wife and children. And as of late, the Lord has inspired me to write such works as this which you are reading now.

While 2011 was a very bad year for me, it turned out to be the best year of my life, for it brought me and my family to the service of the Lord. My children have become very well mannered from attending church, and my wife has donated many of her beautiful quilts that she designs and sews to those in need.

You may think after reading this that our experiences have been horrible and unique, but don't pity us. The only thing that makes us unique from the millions of households across America is that we have evicted the demons that tormented us. Many still live with them, whether they realize it or not.

And as for the demons who say that I owe them, I have officially filed bankruptcy on my debts to them. I have been washed in the blood of Jesus Christ and will be eternally thankful for His sacrifice, that a miserable sinner such as myself could one day join Him in paradise forever and all eternity. Amen.

Chapter 9

THE UNITED SINS OF AMERICA

AVING TOUCHED ON the topic of common sins in America, I would like to further discuss the sins that connect all of us from coast to coast. If we are to believe a city would be destroyed by God for its sin, such as Sodom and Gomorrah, we should believe that any location could be a possible candidate for the same. And as the sins have become the same from state to state and coast to coast, there is little chance that any spot in our entire nation is safe from judgment.

As we know, the Bible says, "The wages of sin is death" (Rom. 6:23)—and many people in our nation are working overtime to earn that wage. Many of us fall into sinful habits and routines and quickly forget that they are sins. Soon the sinful practices are an everyday part of our life, and the more time that passes, the more we forget that we are sinning and the more excusable other sins become.

We must also realize that the more we continue to sin, the more we are actually promoting a sinful way of life.

Not only do we set an example for our children, but also for our peers and everyone that we come into contact with in our lives. I cannot stress enough the importance of fasting from entertainment and ultimately giving it up. We will be much better off if we receive instruction from the Lord, but we cannot do so if we continue to pollute our eyes and ears with demonic influence.

I have created a little story that serves as a good example. This story begins with a demon named Corruption. He was given authority to influence all he could in the atmosphere of his appointed location. Feeding on the destruction of flesh and the damnation of souls, he was a glutton and was always hungry for more. While he was patient, influencing people a little more each day, he always demanded major results before he was finished with them.

One man Corruption had major influence on was Troy, a forty-year-old construction worker who lived in the suburbs with his wife and two kids. Corruption had gained influence over Troy through Troy's love of entertainment. In Troy's mind, there just wasn't anything better after a long day of work than to sit down and watch TV with a few cold beers. His genre of choice had long ago become horror, but he also loved a good action film. And while he certainly wasn't a devil-worshipper, or anything close, he wasn't living according to his upbringing in church.

The evidence of Corruption's influence on Troy was obvious, as he would always praise the latest movie he viewed and describe how it had just enough blood and gore. He also progressed in his use of profanity. Where he once only cursed around his co-workers, he now cursed in public places, in front of women and children, and even at his own children when they came between him and the view of his TV. He would at times complain about a film if it didn't have enough gore or nudity, and he would often say, "There just weren't enough people killed in the film!"

Troy considered himself an outstanding citizen, as he obeyed the law, paid his taxes, and was a positive member of the community by going to work every day. And according to the laws of this world, he was indeed a good citizen. But the laws of the Most High, he disregarded. And little did he know that a demon had influenced him and therefore gained power that could be used against him.

Troy would often complain about not having enough action in his life. He would consider the secret agent in the latest film a god because of the number of women he would sleep with and the amount of people he would kill. He began to hold his wife to the standards of the supermodels depicted in the films, often degrading her by making statements such as, "Why don't you look that good?"

But every morning, when the alarm would ring, Troy would start another day of work the same as the last. He was well grounded and knew the difference between fantasy and reality, but he still wished that if anyone were listening, they would grant his wish for an exciting change in his life. But he certainly wasn't holding his breath. While he had a nice home and truck and a very attractive wife whom he loved, the themes of his entertainment always suggested there was so much more to life and that his was less than interesting.

Now, another man that the demon had heavy influence on was Charles, a thirty-year-old petty drug dealer who didn't know the difference between fantasy and reality. Often high on various drugs, Charles would sometimes forget where he was—or even *who* he was. His addiction to drugs started when he was a teenager and only worsened in his twenties. He also had a love of entertainment, but his choice of poison was pornography.

Many of the role models in his favorite film genre would put any secret agent in any action film to shame when it came to adding up the women they had been with. He was more than addicted to pornography, and it made him view society as a melting pot of men and women who constantly engaged in sexual intercourse, even within moments of meeting as strangers.

Charles started selling drugs after he lost his job upon failing a drug test. While selling drugs provided him enough income to pay for his small apartment and food to get by on, he mainly started selling because he knew he would receive sexual favors from beautiful young girls in exchange for occasionally supporting their drug addiction.

Charles' father had killed himself when Charles was only five years old, and his mother became an alcoholic due to the tragedy. He grew up watching his mother become intoxicated night after night, and she brought strange men into the house on a regular basis. Having no one to guide him, Charles actually appreciated the freedom, as some of his friends in school often complained about the strict and unfair rules of their parents.

Upon the death of his mother when he was twenty-four, Charles had no one in the world to confide in. When he needed guidance, no one was there. And when he would seek guidance from one of his few friends, they would both be too high by the end of the conversation to remember what they had discussed.

He was arrested multiple times for drug charges, breaking and entering, and DWI, and his sentence was scheduled for less than a week away. Having made bail, thanks to his supplier, who wanted him to continue his purchase and sale as long as he could, Charles knew that his time as a free man would soon be finished.

On a midsummer Tuesday morning, he woke up in a heap of dirty laundry, where he had passed out the night before. He was greeted by the voice of a friend, Jeff, who asked, "Do you have any gin or vodka?" Charles had known Jeff for a few years and had met him at a party, where he was selling speed.

"Nope, I think I'm totally dry, man," Charles said. "No alcohol left whatsoever."

"Charles, my man, you only have three days left to celebrate your freedom and you have no alcohol?"

Jeff's statement froze Charles in his tracks. He had forgotten his sentencing was so close. He dashed to the calendar to verify Jeff's statement and saw that he was correct. This bitter reminder put Charles in a panic, so he began to search the apartment for any remaining drug that would help him calm his nerves.

First, as he was pushing aside random trash on the kitchen counter—as empty food wrappers, empty beer cans, filthy dishes—he discovered three pills, each different in color. The pills weren't something he sold, so they had to belong to someone who had been over for a party and left them behind.

"Score!" he yelled as he tossed them in his mouth, followed by a small drink of what was left in a nearly empty bottle of rum. Then he continued his hunt in the living room, as he wasn't sure of the effect of the pills or if they would do the trick.

Jeff recommended they share the meth he had left from the previous night. And so they did, and this put Charles in his comfortable place: on the couch watching porn.

Having sat quietly for half an hour, Charles looked over at Jeff and asked, "Did you drive your car here?"

"Yeah. Why?"

Charles stood up. "Because we need alcohol, my friend! I suggest we go to the store, buy all the alcohol we can afford, and take a road trip to celebrate the remaining time I have left."

"Yes!" Jeff quickly agreed as he dug in his pocket for his keys and headed for the door. They were in his car and on the road in no time.

Having little money—just enough to get them drunk— they talked in the car and decided they would need to choose a store they could easily steal a few bottles of whiskey from, since they planned to include some women in their party. The nearest liquor store was out of the question, as the owner had so often caught thieves and had a shotgun behind the counter. They decided the grocery store a few miles away was their best option—not only had Charles successfully stolen alcohol there before, but in the chance that they did get caught, the highway was only two blocks away. And if the police were called, by the time they arrived, Charles and Jeff would be miles away, beginning their carefree road trip.

Before arriving at the grocery store, they made a pit stop at another dealer's house who owed Charles a favor. There, they each took several hits of meth, and Charles also did a few lines of cocaine, which he chased with a beer in only two drinks.

By the time they were standing in line at the checkout of the grocery store, the combination of the drugs had fully gripped Charles. He was laughing inside at the fact that they were buying thirty dollars' worth of alcohol, while hidden in his pants was more than forty dollars' worth of alcohol.

Suddenly, someone was standing behind him in line. He could smell a delightful perfume that seemed to increase the sensation of his high. He turned slightly and recognized the woman. He didn't know her, but he had seen her at the store before and never had the nerve to talk to her. He remembered her because she reminded him of a particular porn star he so desired. He said to himself, *This is my lucky day. With my last few days as a free man, I am going to have some fun.*

With the combination of a boost of self-esteem from the drugs and a lack of concern for any consequences, he asked her, "So, what's your name?"

She looked away and didn't answer when she smelled the overwhelming amount of alcohol on his breath.

"So, what are you doing today?" he asked.

She answered, "I'm not drinking, that's for sure."

"So, what, do you think you're too good to have a drink with someone like me?"

Again she didn't answer, so he turned around and shrugged, as though her ignoring him wasn't a big deal.

But it was. It served as yet another rejection by the society that would soon lock him away in prison. And it stirred up memories of how his mother had welcomed so many strangers into his home for sex, yet this woman acted as though she was too good to even speak to him, which implied that his mother was a worthless whore.

The woman's cell phone rang with the ringtone of a rock song he had so often heard while partying. This implied to him that she did like to party, just not with him.

As he listened to her conversation, he heard her say something about the money she was going to pick up from the house on her way to the bank. A lightbulb came on in his head, and after checking out, he set a quick pace for Jeff as they walked to the car. When they got in, Charles informed Jeff that the woman behind them in line mentioned something about a lot of money at her house, where she was going after the store.

While she didn't actually say "a lot of money," Charles knew this would motivate Jeff to go along with his plans, as his motives were that of lust. And with money being of no use where he was going to be for the next ten years, he told Jeff he could have it all for himself. So they waited for the woman to come out of the store.

As she walked to her car, she took no notice of them, as she was still on the phone and was also distracted by the greeting of a friend.

As they followed behind her on her way home, Charles began to heavily drink the gin he had just stolen. With the thoughts of cheap porn plots in his head, he wondered how it would play out. Was she playing hard to get? And would she take pleasure in seeing him knock on her door? Would she anxiously invite him in?

As she pulled her car into the driveway, the garage door opened and quickly closed behind her. This gave Jeff the opportunity to park his car right in front of her house without her even noticing.

"OK, here's the plan," Jeff exclaimed. "I'm gonna search the house for everything of value while you get the money and keep her distracted, OK?"

Charles smiled and nodded his head. They got out of the car and walked up to the door and rang the bell. She opened the door with a look of shock on her face, and Charles said, "Hey, babe. Can I come in?"

She yelled "I'm calling the police!"

She began to shut the door, but Jeff lunged forward and burst through as it was nearly closed. She fell to the floor as Charles closed the door behind them. Jeff gave him a thumbs-up and headed upstairs to begin his treasure hunt.

At this point, the demon named Corruption was certain Charles was committed to his will. And in Charles' drug-induced state, the demon took total control of him.

As you can imagine, as in the case of so many headlines we read in disbelief today, Charles raped and murdered the woman, who happened to be Troy's wife. And when Troy came home from work and found her lifeless body in a gruesome scene that wasn't on TV but rather on his living room floor, he took his own life in a sudden loss of sanity.

From this story, we see that the very things that entertain us and bring us a false sense of happiness are the same things that bring us sorrow and destruction. You wouldn't buy ice cream from an ice cream truck that also made and sold rat poison, would you? Likewise, we should not endure entertainment that is possibly tainted with demonic influence. If there is any question, it should be avoided for the sake of your soul.

I feel that we can clearly discern what is proper and what is not if we pray for the Lord to open our eyes and be with us always. If you have the Lord with you, then you know how good you feel and will be able to tell the difference when He doesn't follow you into the video store to purchase that latest zombie thriller or provocative action film that promotes murder, gore, and sexual promiscuity.

Let's take a look at the Ten Commandments for a refresher on the sins that are forbidden us. Many people today are more likely able to recite a Hollywood script than the commandments of God. I have included a reference to these commandments as they are broken in America today.

The Ten Commandments (Exodus 20:3–17)

1. Thou shalt have no other gods before me

Pastor Dwight L. Moody, in the mid-1800s, said this about America: "You don't have to go to heathen lands today to find false gods. America is full of them. Whatever you make most of is your god. Whatever you love more than God is your idol." Rich and poor, learned and unlearned, all classes of men and women in America today are guilty of this sin. If we spend 95 percent of our time watching entertainment and only 5 percent of it studying God's Word, this qualifies. As with many things, moderation must be exercised. For example, if we spend two hours waxing our car and then twenty minutes admiring it, what is God to think when we only have the time at the end of the day to squeeze in a thirty-second prayer?

2. Thou shalt not make unto thee any graven image

Today, there are graven images everywhere we look— statues of political figures, angels, mythological creatures, dogs, cats, and more, plus signs and icons of advertisement for music and film idols. Catholics in America and worldwide, including the Pope, bow down to worship the statues of the Virgin Mary. Many other religions practiced today also bow down to statues of their chosen "god" as well.

3. Thou shalt not take the name of the Lord thy God in vain

Throughout both film and musical entertainment, taking the Lord's name in vain has become a part of mainstream language. This is yet another good example of the need to take extreme caution when viewing entertainment. Curse words that profane the name of God can be found in movies that are promoted to be family-friendly. You may hear your children or even yourself slip up and take the name of the Lord in vain in a sentence, too, because the entertainment has put it into your vocabulary. "OMG" has become such a catchphrase that few people even realize that they are taking the name of the Lord in vain when they use it.

4. Remember the Sabbath day, to keep it holy

With a population of more than 7 billion people on the earth today, it is hard to imagine how hectic shopping would be if stores were not open on Sunday. In a twenty-four-hour-a-day society, many people are forced to work on the Sabbath, whether or not they are comfortable doing so. Is it possible today to keep the Sabbath holy with so much going on? Of course it is—it's only a matter of adjusting our schedule to the will of God.

5. Honor thy father and thy mother

As we honor God, we need to also honor our parents. Many children grow up today with little regard for what their parents have to say. We know that America today forbids that we discipline our children, even though God said, "He who spareth the rod, hateth his son" (Prov. 13:24). The evidence of sparing the rod has proven to haunt us.

6. Thou shalt not kill

Though our homicide rate is under 20,000 murders a year, the more than 1 million babies aborted yearly in this nation are not considered a factor in murder statistics. Mostly, this is because abortion has been considered a legal operation for many decades. It has become considered as no more important than a trip to the dentist to have a bad tooth removed. And with the promotion of murder in our entertainment, we have become less and less likely to consider the value of human life.

7. Thou shalt not commit adultery

Jesus said that whosoever looks at a woman to lust for her has already committed adultery with her in his heart and that if your eye causes you to sin, pluck it out because it is better that your eye should perish, than for your whole body to be cast into hell (Matt. 5:27–29). So, if we are lusting after sex symbols on TV or in pornography, this too is considered adultery.

Jesus also said that whosoever divorces his wife for any reason except sexual immorality causes her to commit adultery (vv. 31–32). As we know, the current rate of divorce in America is almost 50 percent, so there are obviously a multitude of people committing adultery in our nation.

8. Thou shalt not steal

In recent years, a new event has emerged called a "flash mob." A group of people, usually ten or more, assemble in a public place and create a sudden distraction of the public. Some groups, however, have begun creating these distractions in order to steal from stores. Known as "flash robs," it happens when a large group of people runs into a store and steals anything they can grab and then are gone before any action can be taken.

According to the FBI, there were 2.1 million burglaries in 2010, which was a decrease of 2 percent over 2009. There were also an estimated 737,142 auto thefts in 2010 and an estimated 6,185,867 larceny thefts.

9. Thou shalt not bear false witness

It is well accepted that we should lie in America for the sake of money, political gain, advancement in society, and just about any other reason that could be thought of. We know that many often lie to hide a sin, but all of us know someone who lies just for the sake of lying—and they take much pleasure in doing so.

10. Thou shalt not covet

While this tenth commandment is considered by many to be the least of them all, just as it is last, it is just as important to keep and just as broken as the rest. We often find ourselves saying, "I gotta have one of those!" This isn't necessarily a sin, but when we begin to envy a person and meditate on the reasons they have something that we don't, it surely becomes a sin.

And so with all the commandments of God that we break on a daily basis. Across the entire nation, we are united in our sins. We must become ever-familiar with God's laws and elevate to a level of confidence that not even the devil himself can convince us to sin. When we accomplish this, we will be able to help our fellow citizens do the same. While all of us suffer temptation on a daily basis, only those of us who resist will be found in the kingdom of God.

Chapter 10

NOW IS THE TIME TO PREPARE

WHEN WE GET ready for work or school, there is a basic process of events that always unfolds. We first identify that it is time to prepare by looking at the clock. Then we fully wake up and get out of our beds. Next, we put on our clothes and our shoes and inspect our appearance in the mirror. Once we have done this, we eat some food for breakfast. Last but not least, we fasten ourselves into our mode of transportation to get where we need to be.

So, if we first "look at the clock," prophetically speaking, we can determine that the time to prepare is here. Having identified that, we must fully awaken and take the next necessary actions. Just like putting on our clothes, we must put on our armor of God and continually inspect ourselves to keep free of sin. And just like eating our food, we must partake in the Word of God and let it fill us. Last but not least, we fasten ourselves to our mode of transportation, which is Jesus Christ, and let Him take us where we need to go.

While the most important thing we need to do is to become spiritually prepared, we cannot forsake our body, for it is the temple of the Holy Spirit. Many people assume they will somehow be an exception if a famine were to befall us—that somehow they would not starve to death in the events of a severe food shortage. But the signs are all around us that very troubling days are approaching. Why not be ready when it happens?

If you can only afford to buy an extra can of food a week, that would be four cans a month that you have saved for the events of a dreadful scenario. If widespread terror suddenly gripped our nation and it was unsafe to even step outside your door, you would be very happy you had something to get you by till the madness had subsided. The same goes for water, as we know we can only survive a matter of three days or so without it.

We have heard concern and speculation regarding terrorists poisoning our water supply. If this were to happen in a large city, the water could be contaminated for an undetermined amount of time and bottled water would fly off the shelves of every store that sells it within a matter of a few hours. Now, if this actually happened, a case or two of bottled water sitting in your basement would instantly become bricks of gold.

It has been said before, "It is better to have and not need than to need and not have." And this would be a sobering realization for multitudes of people if a catastrophic event were to unfold. If you find that your pantry has filled up faster than you thought it would or feel you have an adequate supply for your family, you can always feed someone else who is in need.

When Jesus returns to rapture the church, many Christians will be surprised at the fact they remain. Likewise, there will be many people starving that thought they would be fed. While many will kill and steal to feed their mouths, adding chaos to an already fragile situation, there will also be many who simply give up their will to live, no longer being fed by the government that they had become so dependent upon.

So, what is the best evidence that we are living in the end times? And, since many past generations have been certain they would see the end and did not, what does that say for those who claim we will see the end today?

First, every day that passes brings us closer to the fullness of time. It is an undeniable fact that we are closer than ever. Second, there is a quickening taking place—all the troubles of the world are intensifying at the same time. Third, when Jesus described the end times to the disciples, had any of us today been standing there listening, it would have been the same story if we were describing our generation to them:

> "And you will hear of wars and rumors of wars. See that you are not troubled; for all these things must come to pass, but the end is not yet. For nation will rise against nation, and kingdom against kingdom. And there will be famines, pestilences, and earthquakes in diverse places. All these are the beginning of sorrows."
>
> —MATTHEW 24:6–8, NKJV

We have seen many great wars, and in the last decade, we have heard many rumors of wars breaking out, even while we were currently engaged in numerous wars. Deadly earthquakes around the world seem to be only more and more common. And there have been famines for many years that have claimed countless lives as well. All these things are intensifying as the beginning of sorrows. And much like a mother with a child in her womb, on a day she does not know, the water will break and the labor to bring it forth will begin. Where we stand right now, it kind of feels like we're nine months pregnant, doesn't it? We have been watching the belly swell larger and larger, and we know there will soon come a point in time when it can swell no more.

We also know that the Lord will pour out His Spirit on the whole earth in the last days before the harvest and that the gospel will be preached around the world as a witness to all nations. I am certainly a witness to this, as well as many others I personally know. In my thirty-one years on earth, it shames me to say I never felt the Spirit of God until this past year. To my surprise, several of my old drinking buddies that I had not seen in many years have since told me they, too, have had the same experience themselves within the last year.

And we certainly know the gospel is being preached around the world through missionaries and traveling ministers and on TV, the Internet, and the radio. Everything that is happening in our world today will soon lead us to the greatest tribulation the world has ever seen or will ever see. And the Lord is certainly working miracles, reaching the hearts of sinners everywhere before the great shaking begins. We must be strong in our faith so that we are still standing after all that can be shaken has been shook.

If you knew without a doubt that the world was literally about to come undone, would you really want your last few days or weeks to have been spent on the things of this world? Or would you want to be at peace, knowing you have dedicated your time to the will of God? There is certainly an awakening taking place, and many people can sense something coming, but no one seems to know what.

The fact of the matter is, many things are coming, and only our faith and trust in the Lord will give us peace and security. I'm sure that when things get bad, many will be willing to trade their souls for food, television, and the ability to continue what we consider an average lifestyle. Make sure that you are not one of them. This life is but a blink of an eye in the scope of things. There is only one God who will decide where we spend eternity, and it is His laws we must obey.

We must also be careful of the stored foods the government hands out in the event of a major disaster. There are many verses in the Bible that describe men having pains like those of a pregnant woman. This sounds to me like salmonella food poisoning, as I have had it before. If there has been cross-contamination and many people are eating directly from the can without cooking the food in the can, this could be a bad scenario.

Many people, as we speak, are preparing in vain by building what they consider indestructible underground shelters. Some pay hundreds of thousands of dollars to fool themselves into believing that they do not need God to help them. But I say that a man who has solid walls and a five-year food supply has less of a chance than a man who has God and one can of beans.

If there is something in your life that you question, you should certainly ask the Lord about it. And if you're not sure you have received a clear answer from Him, get rid of it! It may be the very thing hindering your prayer. And with the hour being so late and the terrible things coming on the earth, I'm sure it's not even worth asking about.

Just drop it, and ask for forgiveness in the possibility it was wrong.

Let's think of the difference between heaven and earth. Imagine for a moment you won the lottery and you had a choice to make regarding the payment option. You could either have a hundred thousand dollars tomorrow or, if you wait, you could have a hundred million dollars next year. Which would you choose? Sadly, many people today have no patience and would choose the hundred thousand. They would have a good time with it, and by the next year, they would find themselves worse off than when they won the money. Because of their reckless spending, they will have gone further into debt.

So we must be patient and not take so much pleasure in the things of this world. For if we give in to the temptations of sin, we will owe debts hereafter that can only be paid with our souls. And if you truly think about it, there is absolutely nothing on this earth that is worth paying for with your eternal soul. How hot is a summer day? And how much worse is it without water? How long can you hold your hand in a flame? Or your entire body, for that matter?

Hell is waiting for many, and many shall it receive. The devil and his angels have been sentenced and given their reservations. They do not want to suffer eternity alone. In their desperate attempt to take the masses down with them, they have made many sins appealing to the eye. And many sinners have been convinced they are not sinners. If we truly beheld a vision of hell, there would be no question—we would run to church and fear God and praise Him all the day long.

It is my hope in writing this book that it find you in the presence of the Lord. But if it finds you where I was not long ago, it is my hope that it might open your eyes to the evils around you and that you might take an inventory of the possessions you own in your home. You may find they are demon possessions and that they have been heavily influencing your life and disrupting your relationship with God.

And let us remember that He said, "I, the Lord thy God, am a jealous God" (Exod. 20:5). So we must not deprive our Creator of His worship, which only He is worthy to receive. Think of the joy we feel when our own children are happy to spend time with us and when we see them come home through the door of our house. Likewise, the Lord is surely pleased to see us come home through the door of His church.

In the works of Josephus,[1] he depicts an image of Hades as a subterraneous region, where the light of this world does not shine. This region is allotted as a place of custody for souls, and after the death of a sinner, they make their descent into this place. Upon their arrival, they are dragged by force by fierce and mighty angels assigned to them, who shall threaten them with their terrible looks. They then experience many tortures within the sight of the unquenchable fire that God has set aside for the day of judgment.

Please trust me—you do not want to see a demon, or even feel the presence of one near you. It is a fearful experience that leaves you feeling lost and utterly hopeless, as I did. But thankfully, I had a seed planted in me that was sown by my family, and I realized I was not hopeless. Jesus Christ died and rose from the grave so that whosoever would repent of their sins and accept Him into their heart as their Lord and Savior might escape all these things.

We are on a battlefield that is choked with an evil

enemy. If we do not stand up and put on our armor of God, we will be overrun by the destructive forces of sin. This, of course, means that we must cross enemy lines and save all of our own who have been taken prisoner by the temptations and sins of the world. We must build up our faith like a soldier who has physically trained for war. We must be full of the Word of God, just as the soldier who has unlimited ammunition. When was the last time a Christian walked into a bar and convinced a sinner to go home to his or her family? When was the last time a man of God stood outside a strip club and warned of the dangers of sin?

What would be our answer if Jesus asked us why we never did these things? Would we say we didn't do it for the fear of being arrested? Or being offended? There are many He could name that have experienced both these things for His name's sake, so we wouldn't have a substantial answer for Him.

We cannot go on being timid or fearful of evil. The hour is too late, and the enemy has surrounded us. We are about to witness the most dramatic world events that have ever taken place on the earth. Let us be strong and optimistic and help as many people as we can, in any way that we can.

In closing, I thank you for taking the time to read. And I hope and pray that this book might inspire you or someone you know to give up their life of sin and seek the Lord Jesus Christ. And one day, possibly sooner than we think, we will all gather together in heaven and eternally share the joy of being in the presence of the Lord. Amen.

NOTES

CHAPTER 1

1. Wikipedia, "History of Television," http://en.wikipedia.org/wiki/History_of_television (accessed March 1, 2013).

2. Statistic Brain, "Television Watching Statistics," verified February 7, 2012, http://www.statisticbrain.com/television-watching-statistics/ (accessed March 1, 2013).

3. Cassandra Jardine, "Are We Losing Our Children to Television?" *The Telegraph*, January 17, 2008, http://www.telegraph.co.uk/news/features/3635318/Are-we-losing-our-children-to-television.html (accessed March 13, 2013).

4. Donald F. Roberts and Ulla G. Foehr, "Trends in Media Use," *The Future of Children* 18, no. 1 (2008), http://www.futureofchildren.org/futureofchildren/publications/journals/article/index.xml?journalid=32&articleid=55&sectionid=232 (accessed March 13, 2013).

5. Bonnie Miller Rubin, "Young People Spend 7 Hours, 38 Minutes a Day on TV, Video Games, Computer, *Los Angeles Times*, January 20, 2010, http://articles.latimes.com/2010/jan/20/business/la-fi-youth-media21-2010jan21 (accessed March 13, 2013).

6. Leonora Epstein, "Diapers and Video Games: The Grossest Thing You Will Read Today," The Frisky, December 1, 2010, www.thefrisky.com/2010-12-01/diapers-and-video-games-the-grossest-thing-you-will-read-today (accessed March 13, 2013); Justin Rohrlich, "'Call of Duty' Players Answer Call of Nature with Adult Diapers," December 1, 2010, www.minyanville.com/mvpremium/call-of-duty-players-answer/?refresh=1 (accessed March 13,

2013); www.funtechtalk.com/diaper-wearing-gears-of-war
-players-shut-down-tournament/ (accessed March 13, 2013).

7. Wikipedia, "Deadliest Earthquakes on Record," listed
under "Lists of Earthquakes," http://en.wikipedia.org/wiki/Lists_
of_earthquakes#Deadliest_earthquakes_on_record (accessed
March 3, 2013).

CHAPTER 2

1. ABC News, *Good Morning America*, "George Stepha-
nopoulos Interviews Russian President Dmitry Medvedev," April
12, 2010.

2. Huffington Post, "U.S. Poverty: Record 49.1 Million Americans Are Poor According to New Census Measures," November 7,
2011, http://www.huffingtonpost.com/2011/11/07/supplemental
-poverty-measure_n_1080160.html (accessed March 1, 2013).

3. Huffington Post, "Plastic Surgery Spending Is Up, as
Number of Chin Augmentations Surges," April 18, 2012, http://
www
.huffingtonpost.com/2012/04/18/plastic-surgery-spending-up
-2011_n_1435512.html (accessed March 3, 2013).

4. Remnant Resource Network, "The Illuminati Exposed:
John Todd Interview and Commentary," http://www
.remnantradio.org/Archives/audio/SJ/Illuminati-Exposed
-John-Todd-Interview.pdf (accessed March 1, 2013).

5. CBS News, *60 Minutes*, "Dylan Looks Back," December
5, 2004, http://www.cbsnews.com/2100-18560_162-658799.html
(accessed March 1, 2013).

6. BallerStatus.com, "Tupac vs. The Illuminati: Hmmmm ... Is
There More Behind This?" August 24, 2009, http://www
.ballerstatus.com/2009/08/24/tupac-vs-the-illuminati-hmmmm
-is-there-more-behind-this/ (accessed March 1, 2013).

7. *Koresh*, "Michael Jackson Was Murdered," thedoggstar
.com/secret-societies/illuminati/Michael-Jackson-illuminati/
Michael-was-murdered/ (accessed March 12, 2013).

8. Julie Ruvolo, "How Much of the Internet Is Actually for Porn," September 7, 2011, www.forbes.com/sites/julieruvolo/2011/09/07/how-much-of-the-internet-is-actually-for-porn/ (accessed March 12, 2013).

9. The United Families International Blog, "Fourteen Shocking Pornography Statistics," June 2, 2010, http://unitedfamiliesinternational.wordpress.com/2010/06/02/14-shocking-pornography-statistics/ (accessed March 1, 2013).

10. Timothy C. Morgan, "Porn's Stranglehold," *Christianity Today*, March 7, 2008, www.christianitytoday.com/ct/2008/march/20.7.html (accessed March 12, 2013).

11. The Ethics and Religious Liberty Commission, "Pornography," http://erlc.com/issues/quick-facts/por/ (accessed March 12, 2013).

12. Wm. Robert Johnston, "Reasons Given for Having Abortions in the United States," August 26, 2012, http://www.johnstonsarchive.net/policy/abortion/abreasons.html (accessed March 12, 2013).

Chapter 3

1. Wikipedia, "*The Exorcist* (film)," http://en.wikipedia.org/wiki/The_Exorcist_(film) (accessed March 1, 2013).

2. Tim Swartz, "The Mysterious Life and Death of Philip Schneider," UFODigest.com, http://www.ufodigest.com/mystery.html (accessed March 1, 2013).

Chapter 4

1. Wikipedia, "Islam by Country," http://en.wikipedia.org/wiki/List_of_countries_by_Muslim_population (accessed March 1, 2013).

2. Wikipedia, "Islam in the United States" http://en.wikipedia.org/wiki/Islam_in_the_United_States (accessed March 1, 2013).

3. Wikipedia, "Moorish Science Temple in America," http://en.wikipedia.org/wiki/Moorish_Science_Temple_of_America (accessed March 3, 2013).

4. Wikipedia, "Nation of Islam," http://en.wikipedia.org/wiki/Nation_of_islam (accessed March 1, 2013).

5. Wikipedia, "Malcolm X," http://en.wikipedia.org/wiki/Malcolm_x (accessed March 1, 2013).

6. Wikipedia, "Louis Farrakhan," http://en.wikipedia.org/wiki/Louis_Farrakhan (accessed March 1, 2013).

7. Wikipedia, "Jeremiah Wright Controversy," http://en.wikipedia.org/wiki/Jeremiah_Wright_controversy (accessed March 1, 2013).

Chapter 5

1. Wikipedia, "1811–1812 New Madrid Earthquakes," http://en.wikipedia.org/wiki/1812_New_Madrid_earthquake (accessed March 1, 2013).

2. Wikipedia, "New Madrid Seismic Zone," http://en.wikipedia.org/wiki/New_Madrid_Seismic_Zone (accessed March 1, 2013).

3. US Geological Survey, "Historic World Earthquakes," http://earthquake.usgs.gov/earthquakes/world/historical.php (accessed March 1, 2013).

4. Campbell Robertson, "For Arkansas Blackbirds, the New Year Never Came," *The New York Times*, January 3, 2011, http://www.nytimes.com/2011/01/04/us/04beebe.html (accessed March 1, 2013).

5. MSNBC.com, "Up to 100,000 Fish Found Dead Along Arkansas River," January 3, 2011, http://www.msnbc.msn.com/id/40887450/ns/us_news-environment/t/fish-found-dead-along-arkansas-river/ (accessed March 1, 2013).

6. Wikipedia, "High Frequency Active Auroral Research Program," http://en.wikipedia.org/wiki/High_Frequency_Active_Auroral_Research_Program (accessed March 1, 2013).

7. US Geological Survey, "Is the Recent Increase in Felt Earthquakes in the Central US Natural or Manmade?" April 11, 2012, http://www.usgs.gov/blogs/features/usgs_top_story/is-the-recent-increase-in-felt-earthquakes-in-the-central-us-natural-or-manmade/?from=title (accessed March 1, 2013).

8. Wikipedia, "Hurricane Katrina," http://en.wikipedia.org/wiki/Hurricane_Katrina (accessed March 3, 2013).

9. Wikipedia, "April 25–28, 2011 Tornado Outbreak," http://en.wikipedia.org/wiki/April_25%E2%80%9328,_2011_tornado_outbreak (accessed March 3, 2013).

10. Wikipedia, "2011 Joplin tornado," http://en.wikipedia.org/wiki/2011_Joplin_tornado (accessed March 3, 2013).

CHAPTER 6

1. Wikipedia, "Quantitative Easing," http://en.wikipedia.org/wiki/Quantitative_easing (accessed March 3, 2013).

2. Christopher Rude, "The World Economic Crisis and the Federal Reserve's Response to It: August 2007–December 2008," September 2009, http://www.peri.umass.edu/fileadmin/pdf/conference_papers/SAFER/Rude_World_Economic.pdf (accessed March 3, 2013).

3. Annalyn Censky, "QE2: Fed Pulls the Trigger," CNN Money, November 3, 2010, http://money.cnn.com/2010/11/03/news/economy/fed_decision/index.htm (accessed March 3, 2013).

4. Tara-Nicholle Nelson, "2011 to Hit Foreclosure Record: Three Need-to-Knows for Foreclosure Buyers," DailyFinance.com, January 17, 2011, http://www.dailyfinance.com/2011/01/17/2011-to-hit-foreclosure-record-three-need-to-knows-for-forecl/ (accessed March 3, 2013).

5. See video posted to YouTube, "St. Petersburg Police Cutting Up Homeless Tents," http://www.youtube.com/watch?v=LrPdZmPB36U (accessed March 3, 2013).

6. Huffington Post, "Food Stamp Usage Continues Climbing to Highest Level Ever," August 3, 2011, http://www.huffingtonpost.com/2011/08/03/food-stamp-usage-highest_n_917038.html (accessed March 1, 2013).

7. To see the current value of US debt, visit www.usdebtclock.org.

8. Cornelius Frolik, "Firearm Sales Up in 2011," *Dayton Daily News*, August 17, 2011, http://www.daytondailynews.com/news/dayton-news/firearm-sales-up-in-2011-1231765.html (accessed March 3, 2013).

9. *The Economist*, "Europe's Rescue Plan," http://www.economist.com/node/21534849 (accessed March 3, 2013).

10. Hugo Duncan, "Investors Write Off £90bn of Greek Debt in Bid to Prop Up Shattered Economy," http://www.dailymail.co.uk/news/article-2112514/Greek-debt-swap-Greece-seals-bond-deal-slash-public-debt-half-secure-bailout-cash.html (accessed March 3, 2013).

11. Wikipedia, "European Sovereign-Debt Crisis," http://en.wikipedia.org/wiki/European_sovereign-debt_crisis (accessed March 3, 2013).

12. Wikipedia, "Mohamed Bouazizi," http://en.wikipedia.org/wiki/Mohamed_Bouazizi (accessed March 1, 2013).

13. *PBS News Hour*, "Tunisian President Steps Down Amid Protests," http://www.pbs.org/newshour/rundown/2011/01/state-of-emergency-in-tunisia-amid-mass-protests.html (accessed March 3, 2013).

14. *BBC News*, "Arab Uprising: Country by Country—Algeria," http://www.bbc.co.uk/news/world-12482297 (accessed March 3, 2013).

15. *New York Times*, "Abdullah II, King of Jordan," updated September 4, 2012, http://topics.nytimes.com/topics/reference/timestopics/people/a/_abdullah_ii/index.html (accessed March 3, 2013).

16. David D. Kirkpatrick, "Egypt Erupts in Jubilation as Mubarak Steps Down," *New York Times*, February 11, 2011, http://www.nytimes.com/2011/02/12/world/middleeast/12egypt.html?pagewanted=all (accessed March 3, 2013).

17. Fiona MacDonald, "Kuwait's Government Resigns After Months of Protests Against Sheikh Nasser," *Bloomberg*, November 28, 2011, http://www.bloomberg.com/news/2011-11-28/kuwait-s-government-submits-resignation-to-emir-following-demonstrations.html (accessed March 3, 2013).

18. Wikipedia, "2011 Yemeni Revolution" http://en.wikipedia.org/wiki/2011_Yemeni_revolution (accessed March 1, 2013).

19. *The Guardian*, "Muammar Gaddafi Is Dead, NTC Says—Thursday 20 October 2011," http://www.guardian.co.uk/world/middle-east-live/2011/oct/20/syria-libya-middle-east-unrest-live (accessed March 3, 2013).

20. Wikipedia, "Syrian Civil War," http://en.wikipedia.org/wiki/Syrian_civil_war (accessed March 1, 2013).

21. Wikipedia, "Occupy Movement," http://en.wikipedia.org/wiki/Occupy_movement (accessed March 1, 2013).

22. Paul Bedard, "Van Jones Group Plans American's 'Arab Spring' Revolt," *Washington Examiner*, April 6, 2012, http://washingtonexaminer.com/van-jones-group-plans-americans-arab-spring-revolt/article/453666 (accessed March 1, 2013).

23. Matthew Kroenig, "Time to Attack Iran," *Foreign Affairs*, published by the Council on Foreign Relations, http://www.foreignaffairs.com/articles/136917/matthew-kroenig/time-to-attack-iran?cid=ppc-gg-iran&gclid=Cmehw7L78bUCFetAMgodolQADg (accessed March 12, 2013). See also http://

in.reuters.com/article/2013/02/13/iran-nuclear-talks-iaea-idINDEE91C0CF20130213 (accessed March 12, 2013).

24. Adrian Blomfield, "Iran Threatens Pre-Emptive Action Against Israel," *The Telegraph*, February 21, 2012, http://www.telegraph.co.uk/news/worldnews/middleeast/iran/9096419/Iran-threatens-pre-emptive-action-against-Israel.html (accessed March 3, 2013).

25. View the video on YouTube, "Dumitru Duduman—America Is Babylon," http://www.youtube.com/watch?v=9Sgakwldbxu&feature=related.

CHAPTER 7

1. Jackie Craven, "Saddam's Babylonian Palace," About.com Architecture, http://architecture.about.com/cs/countriescultures/a/saddamspalace.htm (accessed March 3, 2013).

CHAPTER 10

1. Flavius Josephus, *The Works of Josephus: Complete and Unabridged, New Updated Edition* (Peabody, MA:Hendrickson Publishers, 1980).

ABOUT THE AUTHOR

WOODROW POLSTON ATTRIBUTES his writing to the inspiration of the Word of God. He is currently working on achieving a certificate of theology from a leading Christian university. Woodrow lives in rural Missouri, with his wife, Miryah, and their three children.

CONTACT THE AUTHOR

http://gearsofprophecy.com